MW01140072

Real World Java EE Night Hacks

Dissecting the Business Tier

Adam Bien (blog.adam-bien.com)

http://press.adam-bien.com

Real World Java EE Night Hacks — Dissecting the Business Tier
by Adam Bien

Cover Picture: The front picture is the porch of the Moscone Center in San Francisco and was taken during the 2010 JavaOne conference. The name "x-ray" is inspired by the under side of the porch :-).

Cover Designer: Kinga Bien (http://design.graphikerin.com)
Editor: Karen Perkins (http://www.linkedin.com/in/karenjperkins)

Printing History:
April 2011 Iteration One (First Edition)

ISBN 978-1-4476-7231-9

Table of Contents

Untitled Document

Foreword

Foreword

Most books for software developers are horizontal slices through some piece of the technological landscape. "X for Dummies" or "Everything you need to know about X." Breadth and lots of toy examples. This book takes a largely orthogonal approach, taking a vertical slice through a stack of technologies to get something very real done. Adam takes as his organizing principle one real Java EE application that is not a toy, and goes through it, almost line-by-line explaining what it does, and why. In many ways, it feels like John Lions', Lions' classic Commentary on UNIX 6th Edition.

One of the problems that people often have when they start looking at Java is that they get overwhelmed by the vast expanse of facilities available. Most of the APIs have the interesting property that the solution to any task tends to be pretty simple. The complexity is in finding that simple path. Adam's book shows a path to a solution for the problem he was trying to solve. You can treat it as an inspiration to find your own simple path to whatever problem you have at hand, and guidance on how various pieces fit together...

James Gosling, Father of Java

nighthacks.com

Preface

My first self-published book, *Real World Java EE Patterns—Rethinking Best Practices*, (http://press.adam-bien.com), has sold far better than expected. Even the complementary project (http://kenai.com/projects/javaee-patterns/) is one of the most successful kenai.com projects with over 400 members. The *Real World Java EE Patterns* book answers many questions I have been asked during my projects and consulting work. The old Java 2 Platform, Enterprise Edition (J2EE) patterns have not been updated by Sun or Oracle, and more and more projects are being migrated from the J2EE to Java Platform, Enterprise Edition (Java EE) without a corresponding rethinking of the best practices. Often, the result is the Same Old (exaggerated) Architecture (SOA for short :-)) or bloated code on a lean platform.

The *Real World Java EE Patterns* book was published about two years ago. Since then, I have received lots of requests for information regarding builds, testing, and performance, and I have received more specific Java EE questions. In addition, my blog (http://blog.adam-bien.com) has become more and more popular. Shortly after publishing every Java EE post (these are the most "dangerous"), my Internet connection comes close to collapsing. (You should know that my server resides in my basement and also acts as my Internet proxy.) It became so bad that I started to publish the posts when I was not at home. The whole situation made me curious, so I started to look for monitoring software so I could see in real time what was happening on my server.

I couldn't find any monitoring software specifically for the Roller weblogger (http://rollerweblogger.org/project/), which is what my blog runs on. Java profilers are too technical, too fine-grained, and too intrusive. Launching a Webalizer (http://www.mrunix.net/webalizer/) job after each post was not viable; it took several hours to process all the logs. Thus, the idea of building my "x-ray" software was born.

I was able to build a prototype in a fraction of a weekend and put it into production. It worked well and was good enough to give me an idea of what actually happens behind the scenes on my blog. The result? There was nothing suspicious going on—Java EE is just more popular than I expected. My server was overwhelmed by human visitors, not bots.

I usually posted monthly statistics about my blog manually, which was unpleasant work. I couldn't write the post at Starbucks, because I needed private access to my server. Furthermore, the process involved lots of error-prone copy and paste. I began to think about exposing all the statistics in real time to the blog visitors, making the monthly statistics obsolete. Exposing the internal statistics via Representational State Transfer (REST) made x-ray a more interesting application to discuss, so I started to write this book in parallel.

As in the case of the *Real World Java EE Patterns* book, this book was intended to be as thin and lean as possible. While writing the explanation of the mechanics behind x-ray, I got new ideas, which caused several refactorings and extensions.

Writing a book about x-ray also solved one of my biggest problems. As I consultant, I frequently have to sign NDAs, often even before accessing a client's building. It is difficult to find the right legal people from which to get permission to publish information about my "real" projects, so it is nearly impossible to write about them. X-ray was written from scratch by me, so I can freely share my ideas and source code. It is also a "real world" application—it has already run successfully for several months in production. X-ray is also "mission critical." Any outage is immediately noticed by blog visitors and leads to e-mails and tweets—a reliable emergency management system :-).

X-ray is a perfect sample application, but it is not a common use case for an enterprise project. The data model and the external APIs are too trivial. Also, the target domain and functionality are simple; I tried to avoid descriptions of x-ray functionality and concentrated on the Java EE 6 functionality instead. I assume readers are more interested in Java EE 6 than request processing or blog software integration.

You will find all the source code in a Git (http://git-scm.com/) repository here: http://java.net/projects/x-ray. To see x-ray in action, just visit my blog at http://blog.adam-bien.com and look in the right upper corner. All the statistics shown there are generated by x-ray.

Feedback, suggestions for improvements, and discussion are highly appreciated. Just send me an e-mail (abien@adam-bien.com) or a tweet @AdamBien, and I'll try to incorporate your suggestions in a future update of the book. I will also continue to cover topics from this book in my blog.

Special thanks to my wife Kinga (http://design.graphikerin.com) for the great cover, Patrick for the in-depth technical review and sometimes-unusual feedback, and my editor Karen Perkins (http://www.linkedin.com/in/karenjperkins) for an excellent review.

April 2011, en route from Munich to Las Vegas (to a Java conference…),

Adam Bien

Setting the Stage

1

Webalizer (http://www.webalizer.org/) wasn't able to process the Apache HTTP server log files in a single night any more. The statistics for my blog (http://blog.adam-bien.com) just looked too good. My blog is served by GlassFish v3 from my home network. Sometimes, the traffic is so high that I have to kill the Apache server to be able to browse the Web or send an e-mail.

My first idea was to split the Apache HTTP server files and process them separately. It would be more an administrative task and not much fun to implement. For a pet project, too boring. Then, I considered using Hadoop with Scala to process the log files in my own private cloud (a few old machines). This would work, but the effort would be too large, especially since the Hadoop configuration and setup is not very exciting. Furthermore, extracting information from Apache log files is not very interesting for a leisure activity.

So, I looked for a quick hack with some "fun factor."

My blog runs on Roller (http://rollerweblogger.org/project/), an open source, popular, Java-based blogging platform. Roller is a Java application packaged as a Web Archive (WAR) that runs on every Java 2 Platform, Enterprise Edition (J2EE) 1.4 Web container, and it's easy to install, run, and maintain. It uses Apache OpenJPA internally, but it does not rely on already existing app server functionality. It is a typical Spring application.

As a Java developer, the simplest possible way to solve my problem would be to slightly extend the Roller application, extract the relevant information from the request, and cache the results.

Gathering the Requirements

The pet project described herein, blog statistics software I call "x-ray," has 24/7 availability requirements. I didn't really gather any other requirements up front. The requirements are obvious, since I am the domain expert, operator, quality assurance department, architect, tester, and developer all in one person. This is a very comfortable situation.

The main difference between a pet project and real world application is the fun factor. Primarily, a pet project should be fun, whereas real world apps need to be maintainable and eventually work as specified. In contrast to the real world application development, during the development of x-ray, no politics were involved. If there were, it would be a sure sign of schizophrenia :-)

Functional Requirements and the Problem Statement

Roller comes with rudimentary statistics already. It shows you the total hit count and all referers. The referers tend to attract spammers, and the global hit count is too coarse grained. Plus, the really interesting features are not implemented by Roller:

- Per-post statistics

- Minutely, hourly, and daily hit rates

- Most successful posts

- Trending posts

- Representational State Transfer (REST) interface

- E-mail notifications

- URL filtering

All the statistics should be available in real time. "Real time" means hourly statistics should be available after an hour and minutely statistics should be available after a minute. A real-time monitor would be compelling and also relatively easy to implement. True real-time statistics would require a connection to each browser window. There is no problem maintaining several thousands of such connections from a modern application server, but my Internet connection is too slow for such a requirement.

So far, I've described only a minimal set of requirements. As the project evolves and the statistics data becomes available, new requirements will evolve.

The problem statement for x-ray can be defined as this: "In order to provide detailed, real–time statistics, the Roller software needs to be extended. In addition, the traffic data needs to be persisted, analyzed, and eventually displayed to the blog reader. The blog owner should have access to finer and more detailed information, such as referers."

Non-Functional Requirements

The real-time computation and availability of statistics could be considered as a non-functional requirement. In our case, real-time feedback is the actual goal and the main differentiating feature. Unfortunately, the Roller application needs to be manipulated to access the statistics, which implies some non-functional requirements:

- The installation should be as non-intrusive as possible. Existing Roller configurations should not be extensively manipulated or changed.

- Roller comes with an extensive set of frameworks and libraries. The Roller extension should be self-sufficient, without any external dependencies.

- The statistics software must not be dependent on a particular Roller version.

- The blog performance should be not affected by the statistics software.

- The availability of the blog must not be affected.

The generic non-functional requirements above were prioritized into the following list in descending order:

- Robustness/availability

- Runtime performance

- Self-monitoring capabilities

- Testability/maintainability

- Easy installation

- Scalability

- Extensibility

- Report performance (for accessing the statistics information via REST)

13

The robustness and availability of x-ray is the most important feature. Gathering of statistics must not affect the blog availability.

Constraints

Roller (http://rollerweblogger.org/project/) ran for over 4 years on GlassFish v2. Recently, it was migrated to GlassFish v3.1, J2SE Software Development Kit (JDK) 1.6, and fully virtualized Oracle Enterprise Linux (which is compatible with Red Hat Linux). GlassFish v3+ (http://glassfish.java.net/) is the Java Platform, Enterprise Edition (Java EE) 6 reference implementation.

X-ray is deployed on GlassFish v3 and so it can leverage all Java EE 6 features without any constraints. Maven 3 (http://maven.apache.org/) is used as a build tool that is executed on Hudson (http://java.net/projects/hudson/) and the Jenkins Continuous Integration (CI) server (http://jenkins-ci.org/).

Roller runs on a single node and there have been no performance problems so far, so clustering is considered optional. It is unlikely that x-ray will ever need to run in a clustered environment. A single-node setup makes caching a lot easier and it does not require any distribution or replication strategies.

The Big Picture

2

It is impossible to design even trivial applications on paper. X-ray proved this assertion. My first idea didn't work at all, but it provided valuable information for subsequent iterations.

First Try—The Simplest Possible Thing

Roller is packaged as a J2EE 1.4 WAR. It requires only a Servlet 2.4-capable Web container. Java EE 6 enables WAR deployment of Java EE 6 components, such as Enterprise JavaBeans (EJB) and Contexts and Dependency Injection (CDI) managed beans. WAR packaging of EJB and CDI components is a part of the standard Java EE 6 Web Profile.

The simplest possible approach to extend Roller with Java EE 6 components would be to upgrade the existing `roller.war` to a Java EE 6-enabled WAR and deploy the extensions as Java EE 6 components. Only a single line in the `web.xml` has to be changed for this purpose. Here's the declaration from the original `web-app`:

```
<web-app xmlns="http://java.sun.com/xml/ns/j2ee" xmlns:xsi="http://
www.w3.org/2001/XMLSchema-instance" xsi:schemaLocation="http://
java.sun.com/xml/ns/j2ee http://java.sun.com/xml/ns/j2ee/web-
app_2_4.xsd" version="2.4">
```

It has to be changed to the Java EE 6 version:

```
<web-app version="3.0" xmlns="http://java.sun.com/xml/ns/javaee"
xmlns:xsi="http://www.w3.org/2001/XMLSchema-instance"
xsi:schemaLocation="http://java.sun.com/xml/ns/javaee http://
java.sun.com/xml/ns/javaee/web-app_3_0.xsd">
```

After making only this change, `roller.war` becomes a full-fledged Java EE 6 application. X-ray services can be packaged and "deployed" as a single JAR file containing CDI managed beans, EJB beans, Java Persistence API (JPA) entities, and other Java EE 6 elements.

The x-ray application can be located in either the `WEB-INF/classes` or `WEB-INF/lib`

15

folder as one or more JAR files. The only difference between these is the class-loading order. The container has to load resources from WEB-INF/classes first, and then it loads from **WEB-INF/lib**. X-ray is meant to be a plug-in, so it should integrate with the existing environment in the least intrusive way. Deployment into WEB-INF/lib is the best fit for this requirement. X-ray can be built externally and just packaged with the existing roller.war application.

Java EE 6, particularly, modernized the Web tier. With the advent of Servlet 3.0, the XML deployment descriptor became optional. You can use annotations to configure servlets and filters and override them with the web.xml deployment descriptor on demand. You can also use both at the same time to configure different parts of the system. A single annotation, @WebServlet, is sufficient to deploy a servlet (see Listing 1).

```java
@WebServlet("/Controller")
public class Controller extends HttpServlet {
protected void doGet(HttpServletRequest request, HttpServletResponse response)
    throws ServletException, IOException {
        response.setContentType("text/html;charset=UTF-8");
        PrintWriter out = response.getWriter();
        try {
            out.println("<html>");
            out.println("<head>");
            out.println("<title>Servlet Controller</title>");
            out.println("</head>");
            out.println("<body>");
            out.println("<h1>Hello</h1>");
            out.println("</body>");
            out.println("</html>");
        } finally {
            out.close();
        }
    }
}
```
Listing 1: Servlet 3.0 Configured with Annotations

The servlet Controller is a placeholder for the actual weblog software and was introduced

16

only to test the bundled deployment in the easiest possible way. The StatisticsFilter (see Listing 2) is a prototype of the intercepting filter pattern, which will extract the path, extract the referer, and forward both to the x-ray backend. The StatisticFilter was also configured with the @WebFilter without changing the original web.xml. Both annotations are designed following the "Convention over Configuration" (CoC) principle. The filter name is derived from the fully qualified class name. The attribute value in the WebFilter annotation specifies the URL pattern and allows the terse declaration. You could also specify everything explicitly, and then the annotation would look like this:

```
@WebFilter(filterName="StatisticsFilter",urlPatterns={"/*"})
```

The wildcard pattern ("/*") causes the interception of every request.

```
@WebFilter("/*")
public class StatisticsFilter implements Filter {

    @EJB

    StatisticsService service;

    public static String REFERER = "referer";

    @Override

    public void init(FilterConfig filterConfig) {}

    @Override

    public void doFilter(ServletRequest request, ServletResponse
response, FilterChain chain) throws IOException, ServletException {

    HttpServletRequest httpServletRequest = (HttpServletRequest)
request;

        String uri = httpServletRequest.getRequestURI();

        String referer = httpServletRequest.getHeader(REFERER);

        chain.doFilter(request, response);

        service.store(uri, referer);

    }

    @Override

    public void destroy() {}

}
```
Listing 2: A Test Servlet Without web.xml

In Java EE 6, servlets, filters, and other Web components can happily co-exist in a single WAR file. They are not only compatible; they are also well integrated. An EJB 3.1 bean or a CDI managed bean can be directly injected into a filter (or servlet). You only have to declare the injection point with @EJB or @Inject, respectively.

In our case, an EJB 3.1 bean is the simplest possible choice. EJB 3.1 beans are transactional by default—no further configuration is needed. Even the declaration of annotations is not necessary. Every EJB 3.1 method comes with a suitable default that corresponds with the annotation: @TransactionAttribute(TransactionAttributeType.REQUIRED). A single annotation, @Stateless, makes a lightweight EJB 3.1 bean from a typical Plain Old Java Object (POJO), as shown in Listing 3.

javax.persistence.EntityManager instances can be directly injected with the @PersistenceContext annotation. In this case, no additional configuration is needed. If there is only one persistence unit available, it will just be injected. This is Convention over Configuration again.

```
@Stateless
public class StatisticsService {
    @PersistenceContext
    EntityManager em;
    public void store(String uri, String referer) {
        em.persist(new Statistic(uri, referer));
    }
}
```
Listing 3: StatisticsService: The Simplest Possible X-ray Backend

The EntityManager is a perfect realization of the Data Access Object (DAO) pattern. With the injected instance you can easily create, read, update, and delete (CRUD) all persistent JPA entities. For the vast majority of all use cases, the direct use of EntityManager is good enough. We'll store the Statistic JPA entity with the uri and referer attributes (see Listing 4). I introduced the id, a technical, auto-generated primary key, so it doesn't have to be produced by the application.

```
@Entity
public class Statistic {
    @Id
    @GeneratedValue
```

```
    private long id;

    private String uri;

    private String referer;

    public Statistic() {/*For JPA*/}

    public Statistic(String uri, String referer) {

        this.uri = uri;

        this.referer = referer;

    }

}
```

Listing 4: Statistic JPA Entity

Getters and setters are optional and not necessary in our case. The introduction of the custom constructor public Statistic(String uri, String referer) "destroyed" the default constructor. Because this constructor is necessary in JPA, I had to re-introduce it.

The JPA specification is also a perfect example of the Convention over Configuration principle. The name of the database table is derived from the simple name of the entity class. Every attribute is persistent by default (see Listing 5). The names and types of the attributes specify the names and types of the database columns. JPA requires you to use a minimal configuration file: persistence.xml. The persistence.xml deployment descriptor is required, but it is short and doesn't usually grow. It is the first deployment descriptor for my "proof of concept" application.

```
<?xml version="1.0" encoding="UTF-8"?>

<persistence version="2.0" xmlns="http://java.sun.com/xml/ns/
persistence" xmlns:xsi="http://www.w3.org/2001/XMLSchema-instance"
xsi:schemaLocation="http://java.sun.com/xml/ns/persistence http://
java.sun.com/xml/ns/persistence/persistence_2_0.xsd">

<persistence-unit name="statistic" transaction-type="JTA">

    <provider>org.eclipse.persistence.jpa.PersistenceProvider</
provider>

    <jta-data-source>jdbc/sample</jta-data-source>

    <properties>

        <property name="eclipselink.ddl-generation" value="drop-and-
create-tables"/>

    </properties>

  </persistence-unit>

</persistence>
```

Listing 5: Minimal persistence.xml with a Single Persistence Unit

GlassFish 3+ comes with a preinstalled EclipseLink (http://www.eclipse.org/eclipselink/) JPA provider. Unfortunately, the Roller application is already bundled with the Apache OpenJPA implementation. X-ray, however, was intended to use the GlassFish default JPA provider, EclipseLink.

Because of the existence of OpenJPA in the WAR file, I specified the `<provider>` `org.eclipse.persistence.jpa.PersistenceProvider` `</provider>` tag to minimize interferences with OpenJPA. This is not necessary in cleanly packaged applications. The lack of the `<provider>` tag causes the application server to choose its preinstalled JPA provider. The fallback to the default provider is another convenient convention.

The property `eclipselink.ddl-generation` controls the generation of tables and columns at deployment time. The content of the `jta-database-source` tag points to a properly configured data source at the application server. For our "proof of concept" purposes, I chose the preconfigured `jdbc/sample` database. It is automatically created during NetBeans (Java EE version) installation.

`persistence.xml` contains only a single persistence unit represented by the tag `<persistent-unit>`. You could define multiple deployment units with various caching or validation settings or even with data source settings. If you define additional `persistence-unit` sections in `persistence.xml`, you also have to configure the injection and choose the name of the persistence unit in the `@PersistenceContext(unitName="[name]")` annotation.

The injection of the `EntityManager` in Listing 3 is lacking an explicit `unitName` element in the `@PersistenceContext` annotation and will not work with multiple `persistence-unit` instances. An error will break the deployment. Convention over Configuration works only if there is a single possible choice.

The method `StatisticsService#store` is the essential use case for our proof of concept:

```
public void store(String uri, String referer) {
        em.persist(new Statistic(uri, referer));
    }
```

`StatisticsService` is an EJB 3.1 bean, so the method store is invoked inside a transaction context. The newly created `Statistic` entity is passed to the `EntityManager` and becomes "managed." The `EntityManager` now holds a reference to the `Statistic` entity and tracks its changes. Because it is deployed as `transaction-type="JTA"` (see Listing 5), every commit flushes all managed and "dirty" entities to the database. The transaction is committed just after the execution of the method `store`.

Deployment of the blog software as a Java EE 6 Web Profile WAR was successful. However, the first smoke tests were not. OpenJPA interfered with the built-in EclipseLink. It was not possible to use OpenJPA or EclipseLink in a Java EE 6-compliant way without awkward hacks. The root cause of the problem was the interference of the existing Java EE 5/6 infrastructure with Spring and OpenJPA. The OpenJPA implementation was managed by Spring, and EclipseLink was managed by the application server. Because OpenJPA was bundled with the application, it was found first by the class loader. The EJB 3.1 bean tried to inject the specified EclipseLink provider, but that failed because the EclipseLink classes were overshadowed by OpenJPA.

After a few attempts and about an hour of workarounds and hacks, I started the implementation of "plan B": deploying x-ray as standalone service.

Next Iteration: The Simplest Possible (Working) Solution

So far, the only (but serious) problem is the interference between the JPA provider shipped with GlassFish, EclipseLink, and the OpenJPA implementation. I could fix such interference with GlassFish-specific class loader tricks, but the result would hardly be portable. Although x-ray will primarily run on GlassFish, portability is still an issue.

Relying on application-specific features can also affect the ability to upgrade to future versions of a given application server. I already had minor issues with porting a GlassFish v2 application, which was packaged in a Java EE-incompatible way, to GlassFish v3 (see http://java.net/jira/browse/GLASSFISH-10496). The application worked with GlassFish v2, but it worked with GlassFish v3 only after some tweaks.

Furthermore, application server-specific configurations, such as class loader hacks, always negatively impact the installation experience. If you use such configurations, your users will need application server-specific knowledge to install the application.

Protected Variations ...With Distribution

My "plan B" was essentially the implementation of the old "Gang of Four" Proxy pattern. Because it isn't possible to access the persistence directly, we have to run x-ray in an isolated GlassFish domain (JVM). A proxy communicates with the persistence in the backend and makes the access almost transparent. My choice for the remote protocol was easy. Two String instances can be easily sent over the wire via HTTP. Java EE 6 makes it even easier. It comes with a built-in REST implementation backed by the Java API for RESTful Web Services (JAX-RS) (http://www.jcp.org/en/jsr/summary?id=311).

21

The simplest possible way to access x-ray in a standalone process, from the implementation perspective, would be to use a binary protocol such as Remote Method Invocation (RMI). RMI would fit my needs perfectly. It comes with the JDK, it is almost transparent, and it is fast. The problem is the default port (1099) and the required existence of the RMI registry. RMI would very likely interfere with existing application server registries and ports. The same is true of the built-in Common Object Request Broker Architecture (CORBA) implementation. Both RMI and CORBA rely on binary protocols and are not firewall friendly.

A true solution to the problem would be to introduce Simple Object Access Protocol (SOAP)–based communication. The Java API for XML Web Services (JAX-WS) (http://jax-ws.java.net/) comes already bundled with every Java EE application server, and it is relatively easy to implement and consume. To implement a SOAP endpoint, you need only a single annotation: `@javax.jws.WebService` (see Listing 6).

```
@WebService

@Stateless

public class HitsService {

    public String updateStatistics(String uri, String referer) {

        return "Echo: " + uri + "|" + referer;

    }

}
```
Listing 6: A Stateless Session Bean as SOAP Service

The implementation of a SOAP endpoint is even easier to implement than a comparable RESTful service. SOAP's shortcoming is the required additional overhead: the so-called "envelope." Also, SOAP can hardly be used without additional libraries, frameworks, or tools.

The structure of the SOAP envelope is simple (see Listing 7), but in the case of x-ray it is entirely superfluous, and the envelope leads to significant bloat. The size of the envelope for the response (see Listing 8) is 288 bytes and the actual payload is only 29 bytes. Just taking the SOAP envelope into account would result in an overhead of 288 / 29 = 9.93, which is almost ten times the payload.

```
<?xml version="1.0" encoding="UTF-8"?>

<S:Envelope xmlns:S="http://schemas.xmlsoap.org/soap/envelope/">
```

```
<S:Header/>

<S:Body>

    <ns2:updateStatistics xmlns:ns2="http://xray.abien.com/">

        <arg0>/entry/javaee</arg0>

        <arg1>localhost</arg1>

    </ns2:updateStatistics>

</S:Body>

</S:Envelope>
```

Listing 7: A SOAP Request

SOAP uses HTTP POST exclusively behind the scenes, which makes the use of any proxy server caching or other built-in HTTP features impossible. Although SOAP can be implemented fairly easily on the server side, it is a lot harder for the client to consume. SOAP consumption is too cumbersome without any libraries, and the available libraries tend to introduce considerable external dependencies. SOAP is also harder to test than a plain HTTP service.

```
<?xml version="1.0" encoding="UTF-8"?>

<S:Envelope xmlns:S="http://schemas.xmlsoap.org/soap/envelope/">

    <S:Body>

        <ns2:updateStatisticsResponse xmlns:ns2="http://
xray.abien.com/">

            <return>Echo: /entry/javaee|localhost</return>

        </ns2:updateStatisticsResponse>

    </S:Body>

</S:Envelope>
```
Listing 8: A SOAP Response

SOAP also encourages the Remote Procedure Call (RPC) procedural programming style, which leads to technically driven APIs and less emphasis on the target domain.

Far better suited for RPC communication is the open source library called "Hessian" (http://hessian.caucho.com/). Hessian feels like RMI, but it communicates over HTTP. It is a lean servlet–based solution.

Hessian is easy to use, simple, fast, and well documented, but unfortunately, it is not a part of the Java EE 6 platform. A small (385 KB) JAR file, `hessian-4.0.7` (http://hessian.caucho.com/), must be distributed to the client and server. A single JAR file is not a big deal, but it has to be packaged with the x-ray proxy and could potentially cause other interferences in future versions. Future Roller releases could, for example, use other versions of Hessian and cause problems.

Back to the Roots

RMI is simple and fast, but it requires a connection over a non-HTTP port such as 1099. It also handles ports and connections dynamically behind the scenes. Furthermore, RMI very likely would interfere with the application server services.

Hessian is similar to RMI but it is tunneled over port 80 and effectively implemented as a servlet. The only caveat is the need for an additional JAR file, which has to be deployed with Roller, as well as the backend x-ray services. It's almost perfect, but the Hessian JAR file could potentially interfere with future Roller versions.

The next obvious option is the use of JAX-RS for the REST communication. JAX-RS comes with Java EE 6. From the consumer perspective, REST looks and feels like a usual HTTP connection. There is no specified client-side API in Java EE 6. All major JAX-RS implementors, however, come with their own convenient, but proprietary, REST client implementation. The use of proprietary REST client APIs requires the inclusion of at least one additional JAR file and has the same drawback as the use of Hessian.

Fortunately, we have to use the HTTP `PUT` command with only two string instances. This makes any sophisticated object marshaling using XML or JavaScript Object Notation (JSON) unnecessary.

The obvious candidate for the implementation of an HTTP client is the class `java.net.URLConnection`. It comes with JDK 1.6 and is relatively easy to use. Unfortunately, `URLConnection` is also known for its connection pooling limitations and problems.

For the proxy implementation, I decided to use plain sockets (`java.net.Socket`) first (see Listing 9). It is easy to implement, test, and extend but it is not as elegant as a dedicated REST client.

```
package com.abien.xray.http;
public class RESTClient {
  //...
```

```
public static final String PATH = "/x-ray/resources/hits";
//…
Socket socket = new Socket(inetAddress, port);

BufferedWriter wr = new BufferedWriter(new OutputStreamWriter
(socket.getOutputStream(), "UTF8"));

wr.write("PUT " + path + " HTTP/1.0\r\n");

wr.write("Content-Length: " + content.length() + "\r\n");

wr.write("Content-Type: text/plain\r\n");

wr.write("\r\n");

wr.write(content);

wr.flush();
//… consumer response
wr.close();
//…
```

Listing 9: Plain Socket Implementation of the HTTP POST

The plain socket implementation should meet our requirements. Furthermore, it can be extended easily, for example, with socket pooling, to satisfy future scalability needs. X-ray is meant to be designed according to the KISS principle (http://en.wikipedia.org/wiki/KISS_principle), so there is no premature optimization of the design, implementation, or architecture.

It turned out that the simplistic socket implementation shown in Listing 9 went into production without any modifications. It is more than good enough. In the majority of all cases, it is faster than 1 ms and in the worst case it takes 10ms. In comparison, the request performance of the Roller software varied from 10 ms to 13 seconds.

The server-side counterpart was far easier to implement. With Java EE 6 and JAX-RS, it boils down to a few annotations (see Listing 10).

```
@Path("hits")
@Interceptors(PerformanceAuditor.class)
@Stateless
public class HitsResource {
      //...
    @POST
    @Consumes({MediaType.TEXT_PLAIN})
```

25

```
   public Response updateStatistics(String url) {

       if (!isEmpty(url)) {

           processURL(url);

       }

       return Response.ok().build();

   }

   //...

}
```

Listing 10: The Server-Side POST-Consuming Method

The @Stateless annotation transforms a POJO into an EJB 3.1 bean. EJB 3.1 beans are especially interesting for the realization of a REST entry point. They are thread-safe, monitored, pooled, and transactional. Transactions are the most interesting feature. The method updateStatistics starts and commits a new Java Transaction API (JTA) transaction on every request. The transaction is transparently propagated to the back-end services. As long as the request is propagated synchronously, it doesn't matter whether it is processed by EJB 3.1 beans, POJOs, or CDI managed beans. The transaction is transparently passed to all participants invoked from the updateStatistics method.

EJB beans, as well as CDI managed beans, can be decorated by interceptors (see Listing 11). An interceptor is suitable for the implementation of cross-cutting concerns. It is similar to a dynamic proxy, whereby the container realizes the transparent "injection" of an interceptor between the consumer and the provider.

```
public class PerformanceAuditor {

    private static final Logger LOG = Logger.getLogger
(PerformanceAuditor.class.getName());

    @AroundTimeout

    @AroundInvoke

    public Object measurePerformance(InvocationContext context) throws
Exception{

        String methodName = context.getMethod().toString();

        long start = System.currentTimeMillis();

        try{

            return context.proceed();

        }catch(Exception e){

            LOG.log(Level.SEVERE, "!!!During invocation of: {0}
```

26

```
exception occured: {1}", new Object[]{methodName,e});

            throw e;

        }finally{

            LOG.log(Level.INFO, "{0} performed in: {1}", new Object[]
{methodName, (System.currentTimeMillis() - start)});

        }

    }

}
```
Listing 11: Performance Interceptor.

An interceptor is activated with a single annotation: `@Interceptors (PerformanceAuditor.class)` (see Listing 10). Interceptor configuration also works with respect to Convention over Configuration. A declaration at the class level activates the interceptor for all methods of the class. You can override this global class configuration by putting the `@Interceptor` annotation on methods or by excluding it with `@ExcludeClassInterceptors` or `@ExcludeDefaultInterceptors`.

The `PerformanceAuditor` measures the performance of all method invocations and writes the performance results to a log file. Performance measurement of the entry points (the boundaries) gives you an idea about the actual system performance and provides hints about optimization candidates.

X-ray Probe

3

The x-ray probe is the proxy "injected" into the Roller application, which gathers the metadata of each request and passes it to the actual x-ray application. Because the probe needs to be packaged with the Roller application, it has to be as non-intrusive as possible.

Dinosaur Infrastructure

Roller 4 is a J2EE 1.4 application, pimped up with Spring. The `web.xml` deployment descriptor is declared as `http://java.sun.com/xml/ns/j2ee/web-app_2_4.xsd`. J2EE is more than 7 years old and was designed for JDK 1.4. Annotations were not available at that time, and dependency injection was only possible with third-party frameworks such as Spring and XML; the configuration was sometimes longer than the actual code. Because of the dated infrastructure, the x-ray probe had to be implemented as a J2EE 1.4 application. The x-ray probe is a typical proxy, so it is not supposed to implement any business logic and it just communicates with the backend.

XML Configuration—A Dinosaur Use Case

The x-ray probe is a proxy and decorator at the same time. It uses the Decorating Filter pattern and an implementation of the `javax.servlet.Filter`, in particular, to intercept all incoming calls. Because of the lack of annotations, the filter has to be declared in the `web.xml` deployment descriptor in a J2EE 1.4-compliant way (see Listing 12).

```
<!- declaration ->
<filter>
  <filter-name>HTTPRequestInterceptor</filter-name>
  <filter-class>com.abien.xray.probe.http.HTTPRequestRESTInterceptor</filter-class>
```

```
<init-param>

  <param-name>serviceURL</param-name>

  <param-value>http://localhost:8080/x-ray/resources/hits</param-
value>

 </init-param>

</filter>

<!- mapping ->

    <filter-mapping>

        <filter-name>HTTPRequestInterceptor</filter-name>

        <url-pattern>/*</url-pattern>

    </filter-mapping>
```
Listing 12: Filter Declaration and Configuration in web.xml

The filter has to be declared first and then it is mapped to a URL. In J2EE 1.4, the name of the filter (`filter-name`) and its fully qualified class name (`filter-class`) have to be configured in the `web.xml` descriptor. The value of the key `serviceURL` defines the REST endpoint and has to be configured properly. The key `serviceURL` is the only configuration parameter that is worth storing in an XML configuration file.

The remaining metadata can be easily derived directly from the class, so the `@WebFilter` annotation would be a more natural place to declare a class as a filter. External configurations such as XML files introduce additional overhead and redundancies. At a minimum, the binding between a given configuration piece in XML and the actual class needs to be repeated. Such duplication can cause serious trouble during refactoring and can be fully eliminated with the use of annotations.

Intercept and Forward

The filter implementation is trivial. The "business" logic is implemented in a single class: `HTTPRequestRESTInterceptor`. The method `doFilter` implements the core functionality. It gathers the interesting data, invokes the Roller application, and sends the data after the request via HTTP to the backend (see Listing 13).

```
@Override

public void doFilter(ServletRequest request, ServletResponse response,
FilterChain chain) throws IOException, ServletException {

        HttpServletRequest httpServletRequest = (HttpServletRequest)
request;
```

```
String uri = httpServletRequest.getRequestURI();

String referer = httpServletRequest.getHeader(REFERER);


chain.doFilter(request, response);


sendAsync(uri, referer);
}
```

Listing 13: Basic Functionality of the HTTPRequestRESTInterceptor

The method `sendAsync` is responsible for the "putting" of the URI and the referer. The method name already implies its asynchronous nature. The REST communication is fast enough for synchronous communication. An average call takes about 1 ms, and worst case is about 10 ms. The actual performance of the Roller application is orders of magnitude slower than the communication with x-ray. A single blog request takes between 50 ms and a few seconds.

Threads for Robustness

The reason for choosing asynchronous invocation is not performance; rather, it is robustness. Potential x-ray bottlenecks must not have any serious impact on the stability and performance of Roller. With careful exception handling, the robustness can be improved, but timeout locks might still occur. The socket communication could get stuck for few seconds until the timeout occurs, and that could cause serious stability problems. Blocking back-end calls could even cause uncontrolled threads growth and lead to `OutOfMemoryError` and a server crash.

A decent thread management solution comes with JDK 1.5. The `java.util.concurrent` package provides several robust thread pool implementations. It even includes a builder called `java.util.concurrent.Executors` for the convenient creation and configuration of thread pools. Preconfigured thread pools can be easily configured with a single method call. The method `Executors.newCachedThreadPool` returns a "breathing" `ExecutorService`. This particular configuration would fit our needs perfectly. The amount of threads is automatically adapted to the current load. Under heavy load, more threads are created. After the peak, the superfluous threads get destroyed automatically. This behavior is realized internally—there is no need for developer intervention.

The `newCachedThreadPool` builder method comes with one serious caveat: The creation of threads is unbounded. A potential blocking of the communication layer (for example, Sockets because of TCP/IP problems) would lead to the uncontrolled creation of new threads. This in turn would result in lots of context switching, bad performance, high memory consumption, and an eventual `OutOfMemoryError`. Uncontrolled thread growth cannot be accepted in the case of

31

x–ray, because robustness is the most important non-functional quality and it is the actual reason for using threads.

A hard thread limit, on the other hand, can cause deadlocks and blocking calls. If the maximum number of threads is reached and the thread pool is empty, the incoming calls have to wait and so they block. A solution for this problem is the use of queuing. The incoming requests are put in the queue first, and then they are consumed by working threads. A full bounded queue, however, would lead to blocks and potentially to deadlocks. An unbounded queue could be filled up infinitely and lead to OutOfMemoryError again.

The java.util.concurrent.ThreadPoolExecutor (a more capable ExecutorService implementation) solves the "full queue problem" elegantly. An implementation of the interface RejectedExecutionHandler, which is shown in Listing 14, is invoked if all threads are busy and the request queue is full.

```
public interface RejectedExecutionHandler {

 void rejectedExecution(Runnable r, ThreadPoolExecutor executor);

}
```

Listing 14: The java.util.concurrent.RejectedExecutionHandler

The most suitable recovery strategy in our case is simple yet effective: ignorance. In the case of a full queue and busy threads, all new requests will just be dropped. The rejections are logged and monitored (we will discuss that later), but they are not processed. Unfortunately, there is no predefined builder method in the Executors class with an IgnoringRejectedExecutionHandler. A custom implementation of the ThreadPoolExecutor uses a RejectedExecutionHandler to ignore "overflowing" requests (see Listing 15).

```
 private static void setupThreadPools() {

   MonitorableThreadFactory monitorableThreadFactory = new
MonitorableThreadFactory();

   RejectedExecutionHandler ignoringHandler = new
RejectedExecutionHandler()   {

   @Override

   public void rejectedExecution(Runnable r, ThreadPoolExecutor
executor) {

     int rejectedJobs = nrOfRejectedJobs.incrementAndGet();

     LOG.log(Level.SEVERE, "Job: {0} rejected. Number of rejected jobs:
{1}", new Object[]{r, rejectedJobs});

       }
```

```
};
    BlockingQueue<Runnable> workQueue = new ArrayBlockingQueue<Runnable>
(QUEUE_CAPACITY);
    executor = new ThreadPoolExecutor(NR_OF_THREADS, NR_OF_THREADS,
Integer.MAX_VALUE, TimeUnit.SECONDS, workQueue,
monitorableThreadFactory, ignoringHandler);

    }
```

Listing 15: A Custom Configuration of ThreadPoolExecutor

The method setupThreadPools creates a MonitorableThreadFactory first. It is a trivial implementation of the ThreadFactory interface (see Listing 16).

```
public class MonitorableThreadFactory implements ThreadFactory {

    final AtomicInteger threadNumber = new AtomicInteger(1);

    private String namePrefix;

    public MonitorableThreadFactory() {

        this("xray-rest-pool");

    }


    public MonitorableThreadFactory(String namePrefix) {

        this.namePrefix = namePrefix;

    }


    @Override
    public Thread newThread(Runnable r) {

        Thread t = new Thread(r);

        t.setName(createName());

        if (t.isDaemon()) {

            t.setDaemon(false);

        }

        if (t.getPriority() != Thread.NORM_PRIORITY) {

            t.setPriority(Thread.NORM_PRIORITY);

        }

        return t;

    }
```

```java
String createName(){
    return namePrefix +"-"+threadNumber.incrementAndGet();
}
public int getNumberOfCreatedThreads(){
    return threadNumber.get();
}
}
```

Listing 16: A Monitorable ThreadFactory

The only responsibility of the `ThreadFactory` is custom naming and counting of created threads. Threads created by the custom `Executor` should be distinguishable from threads created by the application server. The name of a thread will look like `xray-rest-pool-42` (the forty-third created thread). Proper thread naming is important for monitoring in production and during stress tests. With tools such as VisualVM (http://visualvm.java.net/), thread monitoring is relatively easy. You will always find a bunch of threads running on an application server, so naming your custom threads differently is a good idea.

The class `ThreadPoolExecutor` reuses already-created threads behind the scenes, so threads do not need to be created for each task. An unchecked exception terminates a thread; what immediately initiates its re-creation is provided with `MonitorableThreadFactory` (see Listing 16). New threads are created only until the preconfigured maximum number of threads is reached. Some `ThreadPool` configurations (such as `newCachedThreadPool`) destroy idle threads. Destroyed threads are also created on demand with the `MonitorableThreadFactory`.

We already covered two of the parameters of the constructor: `ThreadPoolExecutor` (`NR_OF_THREADS`, `NR_OF_THREADS`, `Integer.MAX_VALUE`, `TimeUnit.SECONDS`, `workQueue`, `monitorableThreadFactory`, and `ignoringHandler`). The remaining parameters are less interesting and define the core pool size, the maximum size, the keep-alive time, the time unit, and an implementation of the `BlockingQueue<Runnable>` interface.

The creation and configuration of the thread pool was extracted into the `setupThreadPools` method. The `ThreadPoolExecutor` went to production with two core threads, a maximum size of 2, and a maximum queue size of 2. Not a single request has been rejected so far. The `ThreadPoolExecutor` is stored in a static member. Several `Filter` instances share a single thread pool.

JMX or Logging?

I'm in the fortunate situation being the domain expert, the product owner, the developer, and even the operator, all in one person. In such a case, it is a challenge not to become schizophrenic :-). I began to think about the value of systematic logging in such a situation.

In real world projects, logging is obligatory. No one questions it. Log statements are usually written without even thinking about the person who needs to extract the interesting information. In fact, there should be always a stakeholder interested in log files. Without a stakeholder, there is no requirement, and so no justification, for writing logs.

Logs are not very convenient to write, process, and read. For instance, the impact of the configuration of the `ThreadPool`, the number of rejected requests, and the actual performance of the REST communication are particularly interesting at runtime. Such runtime statistics can be logged for post-mortem analysis, but they are not very convenient to access at runtime. Even trivial processing requires `grep` or `awk` commands.

Although I have root access to the server and could influence the log file format, I was just too lazy to `grep` for the interesting information ,so I used a `tail -n500 -f …/server.log` command instead. The `tail` command provides you with only a recent few lines of a log file. I was interested only in the latest output and rarely used the log files for problem analysis. For monitoring and administration purposes, convenient, aggregated, real-time access to the current state of the system is more interesting than historical data.

If you are not interested in historical data, Java Management Extensions (JMX) (http://www.oracle.com/technetwork/java/javase/tech/javamanagement-140525.html) is easier to implement and access than logging. Current JDKs come with `jconsole` and `jvisualvm`. Both are capable of providing real-time monitoring of JMX beans. With the MBean Browser plug-in (https://visualvm.dev.java.net/plugins.html#available_plugins), VisualVM fully supersedes JConsole.

All interesting attributes need to be exposed as getters in an interface that has a name ending with `MBean` (see Listing 17). This naming convention is important; if it is not followed, the class will not be recognized as MBean.

```
public interface XRayMonitoringMBean {
    public int getNrOfRejectedJobs();
    public long getXRayPerformance();
    public long getWorstXRayPerformance();
```

```
    public long getWorstApplicationPerformance();
    public long getApplicationPerformance();
    public void reset();
}
```

Listing 17: Definition of the MBean Interface

The XRayMonitoringMBean interface has to implemented by a class without the MBean suffix (see Listing 17). All getters will be exposed as read-only JMX attributes in the JConsole / VisualVM MBean plug-in. The method reset will appear as a button. The implementation of XRayMonitoringMBean is trivial. It just exposes the existing statistics from the HTTPRequestRESTInterceptor (see Listing 18).

```
public class XRayMonitoring implements XRayMonitoringMBean{

 public final static String JMX_NAME = XRayMonitoring.class.getName();

    @Override
    public int getNrOfRejectedJobs() {
        return HTTPRequestRESTInterceptor.getNrOfRejectedJobs();
    }

    @Override
    public long getXRayPerformance() {
        return HTTPRequestRESTInterceptor.getXRayPerformance();
    }

    @Override
    public long getApplicationPerformance() {
        return HTTPRequestRESTInterceptor.getApplicationPerformance();
    }

    @Override
    public void reset() {
```

```
            HTTPRequestRESTInterceptor.resetStatistics();
    }


    @Override
    public long getWorstXRayPerformance() {
        return HTTPRequestRESTInterceptor.getWorstXRayPerformance();
    }


    @Override
    public long getWorstApplicationPerformance() {
        return
HTTPRequestRESTInterceptor.getWorstApplicationPerformance();
    }
}
```

Listing 18: Implementation of the MBean Interface

An instance of the `XRayMonitoring` class has to be registered at the `PlatformMBeanServer`. It is similar to CORBA or RMI skeleton registration; you have to pass the instance and its unique name. The name, however, has to fit a predefined scheme. It is a composite name that is composed of the actual name and the type separated by a colon (see Listing 19).

```
public class JMXRegistry {
    private  MBeanServer mbs = null;
    public JMXRegistry(){
        this.init();
    }
    public void init(){
        this.mbs = ManagementFactory.getPlatformMBeanServer();
    }
    public void rebind(String name,Object mbean){
        ObjectName mbeanName=null;
        String compositeName=null;
        try {
            compositeName = name + ":type=" + mbean.getClass().getName
```

```
();
            mbeanName = new ObjectName(compositeName);

    } catch (MalformedObjectNameException ex) {

        throw new IllegalArgumentException("The name:" +
compositeName + " is invalid !");

    }

    try {

        if(this.mbs.isRegistered(mbeanName)){

        this.mbs.unregisterMBean(mbeanName);

        }

        this.mbs.registerMBean(mbean,mbeanName);

    } catch (InstanceAlreadyExistsException ex) {

        throw new IllegalStateException("The mbean: " +
mbean.getClass().getName() + " with the name: " + compositeName + "
already exists !",ex);

    } catch (NotCompliantMBeanException ex) {

        throw new IllegalStateException("The mbean: " +
mbean.getClass().getName() + " with the name "+ compositeName + " is
not compliant JMX bean: " +ex,ex);

    } catch (MBeanRegistrationException ex) {

        throw new RuntimeException("The mbean: " +  mbean.getClass
().getName() + " with the name "+ compositeName + " cannot be
registered. Reason: " +ex,ex);

    } catch (InstanceNotFoundException ex) {

        throw new RuntimeException("The mbean: " +  mbean.getClass
().getName() + " with the name "+ compositeName + " not found - and
cannot be deregistered. Reason: " +ex,ex);

    }

    }

}
```

Listing 19: A JMX Registration Utility

The type of the MBean is derived from the fully qualified class name and passed as a string. The JMX name is constructed inside JMXRegistry (see Listing 19). Various exceptions that are caught during the registration are transformed into an unchecked RuntimeException enriched by a human-readable message. The MBean is registered during the server startup.

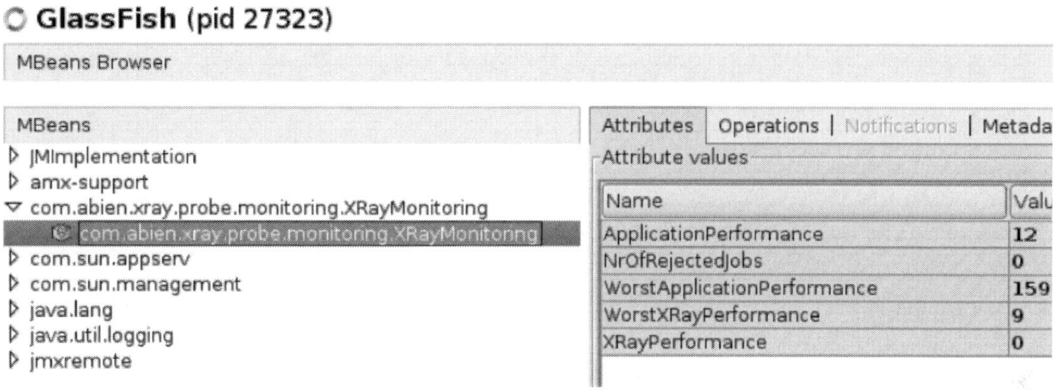

Figure 1: XRayMonitoring MBean Inside VisualVM with MBean Plugin

The usage of the `JMXRegistry` is trivial. You only have to instantiate it and pass the MBean name and the MBean itself to the method `rebind` (see Listing 20).

```
private static void registerMonitoring() {

    new JMXRegistry().rebind(XRayMonitoring.JMX_NAME, new
XRayMonitoring());

    }
```

Listing 20: XRayMonitoring Registration with JMXRegistry Helper

The monitoring values in our example are not automatically updated. To update the recent values, we need to click the "refresh" button in the VisualVM or JConsole user interface. JMX provides a solution for automatic updates. You could use JMX notifications for the implementation of automatic updates. Also, the implementation of bounded or range values is natively supported by JMX with implementations of the `GaugeMonitor` class (http://download.oracle.com/javase/ 1.5.0/docs/api/javax/management/monitor/GaugeMonitor.html).

The `NrOfRejectedJobs` (see Figure 1) attribute would be a good candidate for observation. In case of an increasing number of rejected jobs, `GaugeMonitor` could send notifications (events) proactively. Such events usually cause the creation of emergency ticket e-mails or SMS messages to notify the operators about an issue. The attribute `NrOfRejecteJobs` is particularly simple; every value other zero should be considered a problem.

The Self-Contained REST Client

Obviously, HTTP protocol implementation is not the core responsibility of the `HttpRequestRESTInterceptor`; rather, its core responsibility is the interception of requests and the forwarding of the relevant data to a sink. Although the filter doesn't care about REST, HTTP, or any protocol, the fragment "REST" in the filter name makes the chosen protocol visible in the web.xml configuration. The name was chosen for convenience, not for the actual responsibilities of the filter.

The actual HTTP implementation is fully encapsulated in a self-contained RESTClient class (see Listing 21). It doesn't rely on any external library and instead uses plain old java.net.Sockets. As already mentioned, the performance is good enough; the worst measured response time was around 10 ms. The performance data is exposed through JMX. Keep in mind that the measured performance represents the whole invocation chain, not only the REST communication.

```
public class RESTClient {

    public static final String PATH = "/x-ray/resources/hits";

    private InetAddress inetAddress;

    private int port;

    private String path;

    private static final Logger logger = Logger.getLogger
(RESTClient.class.getName());


    public RESTClient(String hostName, int port, String path) {

        try {

            this.inetAddress = InetAddress.getByName(hostName);

            this.port = port;

            this.path = path;

        } catch (UnknownHostException ex) {

            throw new IllegalArgumentException("Wrong: " + hostName
+ " Reason: " + ex, ex);

        }

    }


    public RESTClient(URL url) {

        this(url.getHost(), url.getPort(), url.getPath());

    }


    public RESTClient() {
```

```java
        this("localhost", 8080, PATH);
    }


    public String put(String content) {
      try {
        Socket socket = new Socket(inetAddress, port);

        BufferedWriter wr = new BufferedWriter(new OutputStreamWriter
(socket.getOutputStream(), "UTF8"));

        InputStreamReader is = new InputStreamReader
(socket.getInputStream());

        wr.write("PUT " + path + " HTTP/1.0\r\n");

        wr.write("Content-Length: " + content.length() + "\r\n");

        wr.write("Content-Type: text/plain\r\n");

        wr.write("\r\n");

        wr.write(content);

            //… exception handling / InputStream -> String conversion
}


        public InetAddress getInetAddress() {
            return inetAddress;
        }


        public String getPath() {
            return path;
        }


        public int getPort() {
            return port;
        }
    }
```

Listing 21: An HTTP POST Implementation in RESTClient

The key functionality is implemented in the method `public String put(String` content) (see Listing 21). The implementation of a PUT request requires only three lines of code. You only have to specify the HTTP method (PUT, in our case), the content length, and the type and then provide the actual payload.

Note the intentional swallowing of exceptions. Inside the catch block, only the content of the exception is logged. Swallowing an exception is uncommon, but it is very effective in our case. Even if the x-ray backend is not available, the x-ray probe will not affect the stability of the blog. All data will be lost during this period of time, but there is no way to process the data correctly without having a fully functional backend in place anyway. The way exceptions are handled is very dependent on x-ray's responsibilities. Imagine if x-ray were an audit system required by a fictional legal department. Then all relevant back-end problems should be propagated to the user interface.

In our case, robustness and performance are more important than the consistency or availability of the statistical data. It is a pure business decision. If I (in the role of a domain expert) decide that absolutely all requests must be captured in real time, then I (in the role of a developer) would need to throw an unchecked exception to roll back the whole transaction. This means that the blog will only function correctly if the x-ray backend is up and running. The decision about how to react to a failure of the put method cannot be made by a developer without asking the domain expert.

HTTPRequestRESTInterceptor at Large

Until now, I discussed various snippets from the HTTPRequestRESTInterceptor. It's time to put all the pieces together (see Listing 22).

Surprisingly, HTTPRequestRESTInterceptor relies on a static initializer to instantiate the threadpools and register the JMX monitoring. References to the thread pool, as well as the JMX monitoring, are stored in static fields. There should be only a single thread pool and JMX monitoring for all HTTPRequestRESTInterceptor instances.

```
public class HTTPRequestRESTInterceptor implements Filter {

    private final static Logger LOG = Logger.getLogger
(HTTPRequestRESTInterceptor.class.getName());

    private String serviceURL;

    private URL url;

    RESTClient client;
```

```java
static final String REFERER = "referer";

static final String DELIMITER = "|";

static Executor executor = null;

private static AtomicInteger nrOfRejectedJobs = new
AtomicInteger(0);

private static long xrayPerformance = -1;

private static long worstXrayPerformance = -1;

private static long applicationPerformance = -1;

private static long worstApplicationPerformance = -1;

public final static int NR_OF_THREADS = 2;

public final static int QUEUE_CAPACITY = 5;


static {

    setupThreadPools();

    registerMonitoring();

}


@Override
public void init(FilterConfig filterConfig) throws
ServletException {

        this.serviceURL = filterConfig.getInitParameter
("serviceURL");

        try {

            this.url = new URL(this.serviceURL);

            this.client = new RESTClient(this.url);

        } catch (MalformedURLException ex) {

            Logger.getLogger
(HTTPRequestRESTInterceptor.class.getName()).log(Level.SEVERE, null,
ex);

        }

    }


    private static void setupThreadPools() {

        MonitorableThreadFactory monitorableThreadFactory = new
```

```java
MonitorableThreadFactory();

        RejectedExecutionHandler ignoringHandler = new
RejectedExecutionHandler()   {


            @Override

            public void rejectedExecution(Runnable r,
ThreadPoolExecutor executor) {
                int rejectedJobs = nrOfRejectedJobs.incrementAndGet
();
                LOG.log(Level.SEVERE, "Job: {0} rejected. Number of
rejected jobs: {1}", new Object[]{r, rejectedJobs});


            }

        };
        BlockingQueue<Runnable> workQueue = new
ArrayBlockingQueue<Runnable>(QUEUE_CAPACITY);

        executor = new ThreadPoolExecutor(NR_OF_THREADS,
NR_OF_THREADS, Integer.MAX_VALUE, TimeUnit.SECONDS, workQueue,
monitorableThreadFactory, ignoringHandler);

    }


    private static void registerMonitoring() {

        new JMXRegistry().rebind(XRayMonitoring.JMX_NAME, new
XRayMonitoring());

    }


    @Override

    public void doFilter(ServletRequest request, ServletResponse
response, FilterChain chain) throws IOException, ServletException {

        HttpServletRequest httpServletRequest =
(HttpServletRequest) request;


        String uri = httpServletRequest.getRequestURI();

        String referer = httpServletRequest.getHeader(REFERER);


        long start = System.currentTimeMillis();
```

```java
        chain.doFilter(request, response);

        applicationPerformance = (System.currentTimeMillis() -
start);

        worstApplicationPerformance = Math.max
(applicationPerformance, worstApplicationPerformance);

        sendAsync(uri, referer);

    }


    public void sendAsync(final String uri, final String referer) {

        Runnable runnable = getInstrumentedRunnable(uri, referer);

        String actionName = createName(uri, referer);

        executor.execute(new ThreadNameTrackingRunnable(runnable,
actionName));

    }


    public Runnable getInstrumentedRunnable(final String uri, final
String referer) {

        return new Runnable()  {

            @Override

            public void run() {

                long start = System.currentTimeMillis();

                send(uri, referer);

                xrayPerformance = (System.currentTimeMillis() -
start);

                worstXrayPerformance = Math.max(xrayPerformance,
worstXrayPerformance);

            }

        };

    }


    String createName(final String uri, final String referer) {

        return uri + "|" + referer;

    }
```

```java
public void send(final String uri, final String referer) {
    String message = createMessage(uri, referer);
    client.put(message);
}


String createMessage(String uri, String referer) {
    if (referer == null) {
        return uri;
    }
    return uri + DELIMITER + referer;
}


public static int getNrOfRejectedJobs() {
    return nrOfRejectedJobs.get();
}


public static long getApplicationPerformance() {
    return applicationPerformance;
}


public static long getXRayPerformance() {
    return xrayPerformance;
}


public static long getWorstApplicationPerformance() {
    return worstApplicationPerformance;
}


public static long getWorstXRayPerformance() {
    return worstXrayPerformance;
}
```

```
public static void resetStatistics() {
    worstApplicationPerformance = 0;

    worstXrayPerformance = 0;

    applicationPerformance = 0;

    xrayPerformance = 0;

    nrOfRejectedJobs.set(0);
}


@Override
public void destroy() {

}


}
```

Listing 22: HTTPRequestRESTInterceptor at Large

Starting threads in an EJB container is prohibited. Starting threads in a Web container is not. Both containers are usually executed in the same JVM process, so constraints regarding the EJB container might seem strange at the first glance. Keep in mind that the Servlet specification is older than EJB. Furthermore, both specifications were developed independently of each other.

Our setup is unusual; we are executing the frontend and the backend in separate JVMs and GlassFish domains. Roller runs as a J2EE 1.4 application and x-ray runs in a Java EE 6 container. REST communication is used to bridge the gap between both processes.

The size of the class `HTTPRequestRESTInterceptor` is about 170 lines of code. The main responsibility of this class is the extraction of interesting metadata from HTTP requests and performance measurements in a non-intrusive way. Profiling and JMX handling are actually not the core responsibilities of the `HTTPRequestRESTInterceptor` class and they should be extracted into standalone classes. On the other hand, `HTTPRequestRESTInterceptor` is feature-complete. Excessive growth in complexity is rather unlikely.

I haven't covered the class `ThreadNameTrackingRunnable` yet. It is a very useful hack. `ThreadNameTrackingRunnable` is a classic decorator, or aspect. It expects a `java.lang.Runnable` instance in a constructor as a parameter and wraps the `run` method with additional functionality. The added value of `ThreadNameTrackingRunnable` is the temporary renaming of the current thread. The name of the thread comprises the name of the action and the original thread name. After the invocation of the actual `run` method, the changes are rolled back (see Listing 23).

```java
public class ThreadNameTrackingRunnable implements Runnable{

    private String actionName;

    private Runnable runnable;


    public ThreadNameTrackingRunnable(Runnable runnable,String
actionName) {

        this.actionName = actionName;

        this.runnable = runnable;

    }

    @Override

    public void run() {

        String originName = Thread.currentThread().getName();

        String tracingName = this.actionName + "#" + originName;

        try{

            Thread.currentThread().setName(tracingName);

            this.runnable.run();

        }finally{

            Thread.currentThread().setName(originName);

        }

    }

    @Override

    public String toString() {

        return "CurrentThreadRenameableRunnable{" + "actionName=" +
actionName + '}';

    }

}
```

Listing 23: Renaming the Current Thread

Thread renaming inside an EJB container is not allowed, but there are no such restrictions in a Web container. Naming threads more fluently significantly simplifies the interpretation of VisualVM and JConsole output, and it even increases the readability of a thread dump. With that trick, it is very easy to monitor stuck threads. You only have to connect to the JVM and list all threads to identify slow actions. ThreadNameTrackingRunnable uses the name of the URI

48

for renaming. Just by looking at the thread dump, you get an idea about what your system is doing.

Sending MetaData with REST or KISS in Second Iteration

The first iteration of the client was simplistic and successfully deployed in production for several weeks. It worked perfectly until a crawling bot found some strange posts interesting and begun to poll these. After a few days, these three posts became the top three and were, by far, the most popular ones.

The robot itself was easily identifiable. The user agent (`tversity mediabot`) in the HTTP header revealed his non-human nature. The remedy is simple: All requests containing the robot's user agent would be monitored but ignored in the statistics. A filter implementation, for example, a single method `boolean accept(String uri)`, would easily solve the problem. The easiest possible solution would be the implementation of the filter logic directly in the x-ray probe. No changes in the backend would be required in that case. Although this solution would work, it has some significant drawbacks:

- Potential performance problems could directly affect the application. Asynchronous processing in the plain Web container is harder to achieve.

- The distribution of business logic is harder to maintain. The x-ray probe should remain a simple proxy.

- Robot activity couldn't be monitored; it would be invisible at the server side.

- For every additional aspect or bug fix, the x-ray probe would have to be recompiled and the application (Roller blog) would need to be restarted.

A back-end filter implementation isn't any harder, but the user agent has to be passed from the client to the server for that purpose. To meet this requirement, the URI and referer encoding on the x-ray probe and server will have to be enhanced to support the additional user agent parameter. The current encoding is not flexible enough. See the following excerpt from Listing 22:

```
String createName(final String uri, final String referer) {
        return uri + "|" + referer;
    }
```

Achieving server-side filtering turned out to be major rework. Encoding of additional key-value pairs in the HTTP body was completely removed and they were passed in an HTTP header instead. For this purpose, the client implementation had to be extended to support the key–value pairs passed in HTTP header (see Listing 24):

```java
public static final String HEADER_NAME_PREFIX = "xray_";

public void put(String content, Map<String,String> headers) {

        try {

            Socket socket = new Socket(inetAddress, port);

            socket.setSoTimeout(TIMEOUT);

            BufferedWriter wr = new BufferedWriter(new
OutputStreamWriter(socket.getOutputStream(), "UTF8"));

            wr.write("PUT " + path + " HTTP/1.0\r\n");

            wr.write(getFormattedHeader("Content-Length","" +
content.length()));

            wr.write(getFormattedHeader("Content-Type", "text/
plain"));

        for (Map.Entry<String, String> header : headers.entrySet
()) {

                wr.write(getFormattedHeader(HEADER_NAME_PREFIX +
header.getKey(),header.getValue()));

            }

        //bookkeeping skipped

    }

    String getFormattedHeader(String key,String value){

        return key + ": " + value + "\r\n";

    }
```

Listing 24: Passing Additional Key Values in a Header

With the availability of key-value pairs, metadata processing and transport become generic. The HTTP headers are converted into a `Map<String,String>` (see Listing 25):

```java
 Map<String,String> extractHeaders(HttpServletRequest
httpServletRequest){

    Map<String,String> headers = new HashMap<String, String>();

    Enumeration<String> headerNames =
httpServletRequest.getHeaderNames();

        if(headerNames == null){

            return headers;

        }

        while (headerNames.hasMoreElements()){

            String name = headerNames.nextElement();
```

```
        String header = httpServletRequest.getHeader(name);

        headers.put(name,header);

    }

    return headers;

}
```

Listing 25: HTTP Header to `java.util.Map` Conversion

Sending the original headers directly via HTTP PUT would break the HTTP communication. Essential headers, such as `Content-Length`, or `Content-Type`, would be overridden. This would cause errors and lead to undefined behavior. To resolve the collisions, the constant `xray_` is prepended to each header name. Sending original headers with encoded names ensures uniqueness and allows the attachment of arbitrary amounts of additional metadata to an HTTP request. The server has access to the entire metadata and can perform arbitrary filtering. The client remains responsible for metadata extraction and communication only.

Don't Test Everything

Unit tests are very capable of finding trivial bugs and misconceptions quickly. At conferences, in blogs, in articles, and in Ivory Towers, 80+% code coverage seems to be a well-established standard.

Using code coverage as a metric is fun in my case (I'm also in the role of the quality assurance department :-)), but it can be very destructive in bigger corporations. Forcing developers to conform to a code coverage statistic causes extensive testing of trivial stuff first. Especially in J2EE projects, you could achieve remarkable code coverage with testing of indirections, layering, and dumb data transfer objects (DTOs), without even touching the actual business logic.

For x-ray, I wrote tests only for methods that have a significant amount of business logic. But should we define "significant"? You can find a good definition for "a significant amount of business logic" in Wikipedia under "cyclomatic complexity" (http://en.wikipedia.org/wiki/Cyclomatic_complexity). Cyclomatic complexity measures the number of independent execution paths in your methods and classes and even in your modules. The higher the number, the higher the complexity. An `if-else` block would result in a cyclomatic complexity of 2. For loops, `while`, and `try-catch` blocks increase the cyclomatic complexity as well. A good rule of thumb is to write tests for everything with a cyclomatic complexity higher than 3.

Therefore, I decided to test only methods with at least a single `if-else` block. Testing of getters and setters is not only unnecessary, but from a maintainability perspective, even counter-productive.

The free Maven plug-in Sonar (http://www.sonarsource.com) comes with a useful visualization of cyclomatic complexity combined with code coverage (see Figure 2). Complexity increases the font size and code coverage influences the font color. Complex, untested classes are shown with big, red letters.

Some of the x-ray classes displayed in Figure 2 appear in red, and they were tested. For example, `Configuration`, `LoggerProducer`, and `DelegatingLogger` were tested with the Maven Failsafe plug-in (http://maven.apache.org/plugins/maven-failsafe-plugin/)outside the Sonar instrumentation. Sonar can also be extended to measure code coverage for integration tests. You will have to install an additional agent in this case (http://www.sonarsource.org/measure-code-coverage-by-integration-tests-with-sonar/).

Figure 2: Sonar -> Clouds -> Top Risks View

This combination of code coverage and cyclomatic complexity is particularly useful for the identification of critical classes. The higher the complexity of a method, the harder it is to test. A single method with many internal decisions and loops is harder to test than several simpler methods. It is even more likely that you will not be able to test a complex method just by varying the object state and input parameters.

The testability can be increased by extracting the blocks into additional, easier-to-test methods. Writing tests for the factored-out methods increases the code coverage and the refactoring decreases the complexity. After only a few refactorings, the tests usually significantly improve the code coverage and decrease the complexity. The recomputation of the complexity statistics happens automatically on every Mercurial hg push or Subversion (SVN) commit—we will cover that later in the Continuous Integration process.

Testing the X-ray Probe

X-ray is a pet project and its primary purpose is to have some fun. For test purposes, we will use ScalaTest (http://scalatest.org/) with Mockito (http://mockito.org/) instead of the well known JUnit 4 (http://junit.org/). ScalaTest can be easily combined with Maven and integrated with Hudson (http://java.net/projects/hudson/).

In the x-ray setup, JUnit is still used to run the test and integrate with Maven. ScalaTest uses the JUnit runner to execute the tests. See Listing 26.

```scala
package com.abien.xray.probe.http

import org.scalatest.junit.JUnitSuite

import org.scalatest.junit.ShouldMatchersForJUnit

import org.mockito.Mockito._

import org.scalatest.mock.MockitoSugar

import org.junit._

import Assert._

import javax.servlet.FilterConfig


class HTTPRequestRESTInterceptorTest extends JUnitSuite with
MockitoSugar with ShouldMatchersForJUnit{
  var cut:HTTPRequestRESTInterceptor = _
  @Before
  def setUp: Unit = {
    cut = new HTTPRequestRESTInterceptor()
  }
  @Test
  def createMessageWithoutReferer = {
    val uri = "/hello/world"
    val referer = null
    val message = cut.createMessage(uri,referer)
    message should be (uri)
  }
```

```scala
  @Test
  def createMessageWithReferer = {
    val uri = "/hello/world"
    val referer = "adam-bien.com"
    val message = cut.createMessage(uri,referer)
    message should be (uri+HTTPRequestRESTInterceptor.DELIMITER
+referer)
  }


  @Test
  def initWithServiceURL = {
    var filterConfig = mock[FilterConfig]
    def expected:String = "http://localhost:8080"
    when(filterConfig.getInitParameter
(HTTPRequestRESTInterceptor.SERVICE_URL_KEY)).thenReturn(expected)
    cut.init(filterConfig)
    cut.url.toExternalForm should equal (expected)
    cut.client should not be (null)
  }


  @Test
  def initWithOutServiceURL = {
    var filterConfig = mock[FilterConfig]
    cut.init(filterConfig)
    cut.url should be (null)
    cut.client should be (null) //malformed URL
  }


  @Test
  def getInstrumentedRunnable = {
    def uri = "/hello"
    def referer = "/hugo"
```

54

```scala
    cut.getInstrumentedRunnable(uri, referer) should not be (null)
  }


  @Test
  def sendAsync = {
    val uri = "http://hugo.com"
    val ref = "localhost"
    cut.client = mock[RESTClient]
    cut.sendAsync(uri, ref)
    verify(cut.client,times(1)).put(cut.createMessage(uri, ref));
    HTTPRequestRESTInterceptor.getNrOfRejectedJobs should be (0)
  }


  @Test(timeout=500)
  def sendAsyncAndOverload = {
    val uri = "http://hugo.com"
    val ref = "localhost"
    cut.client = new RESTClient(){
      override def put(content:String) {
        Thread.sleep(200);
      }
    };
    val overload:Int = 10;
    for(i <- 0 until (HTTPRequestRESTInterceptor.QUEUE_CAPACITY +
HTTPRequestRESTInterceptor.NR_OF_THREADS +overload)){
      cut.sendAsync(uri + i, ref + i)
    }
    HTTPRequestRESTInterceptor.getNrOfRejectedJobs should be
(overload)
  }
}
```

Listing 26: HTTPRequestRESTInterceptorTest—Testing the Hard Stuff

The method `initWithServiceURL` is the easiest to start with. The invocation `mock [FilterConfig]` creates a mock implementation on the fly and is equivalent to the `org.mockito.Mockito.mock(FilterConfig.class)` invocation. The return value is an already usable dummy implementation without any behavior. The behavior is conveniently recorded with the following invocation:

```
when(filterConfig.getInitParameter
(HTTPRequestRESTInterceptor.SERVICE_URL_KEY)).thenReturn(expected)
```

Whenever the method `getInitParameter` is invoked, the `String expected` is returned. A preconfigured `FilterConfig` mockup is passed to the method `init`. Then it is possible to test the actual initialization functionality.

More interesting functionality to test is the overload behavior of the `HTTPRequestRESTInterceptor`. We will attempt to overload the `HTTPRequestRESTInterceptor` by passing more blocking `Runnable` instances than the queue depth and amount of working threads can handle. For this purpose, a `RESTClient` instance with an overridden method `put` is created (see Listing 27). The method `put` blocks for 200ms just to simulate an overloaded x-ray backend. We are computing the number of jobs that can be handled and adding an overload factor. With the computed number, the method `sendAsync` gets invoked. The expected value is the overload factor:

```
@Test(timeout=500)
def sendAsyncAndOverload = {
  val uri = "http://hugo.com"
  val ref = "localhost"
  cut.client = new RESTClient(){
    override def put(content:String) {
      Thread.sleep(200);
    }
  }
  val overload:Int = 10
  for(i <- 0 until (HTTPRequestRESTInterceptor.QUEUE_CAPACITY +
HTTPRequestRESTInterceptor.NR_OF_THREADS +overload)){
    cut.sendAsync(uri + i, ref + i)
  }

  HTTPRequestRESTInterceptor.getNrOfRejectedJobs should be (overload)
}
```

```
}
```
Listing 27: Overriding put Method for Overload

The correct computation of the number of rejected jobs is interesting. More important is the ability to overload the x-ray probe without blocking. The attribute timeout in the annotation `@Test` specifies the maximum number of milliseconds within which the test must pass. A longer invocation causes the test to fail. The timeout constraint prevents the test from blocking and causes a failure instead.

X-ray REST Services

4

The x-ray-services module provides the actual business logic. The business logic processes the URIs with corresponding metadata, and it also offers basic statistic services at the same time. The need to provide the business logic in a dedicated application and an isolated JVM was caused by the incompatibilities with the Roller 4 application, not by scalability or maintainability considerations. Running x-ray inside the same process as Roller would be the easiest and fastest possible choice, but it won't suffice in this case. "Don't distribute" should be considered to be general advice, not an absolute best practice.

Give Me Some REST

X-ray runs on Java EE 6 and Java EE 6 comes with JAX-RS (JSR-311) (http://jcp.org/en/jsr/detail?id=311). "JAX-RS" stands for Java Architecture For XML RESTful Services. It specifies a vendor-neutral API for server-side implementation of RESTful services.

Every Java EE 6-capable application server has to provide a JAX-RS implementation. Because a JAX-RS implementation has to come with every Java EE 6-compliant server, you don't have to deploy a JAX-RS runtime environment with your application. On Java EE servers prior to version 6, you have to provide a JAX-RS implementation with your application and a customized `web.xml` with a configured REST servlet.

JAX-RS is an annotation-based API. The annotation javax.ws.rs.Path binds a class to a particular URL segment after a predefined prefix. The prefix comprises the WAR file name followed by the value of the annotation ApplicationPath (see Listing 28).

```
@javax.ws.rs.ApplicationPath("resources")
public class ApplicationConfig extends javax.ws.rs.core.Application {}
```
Listing 28: Configuration of the REST URL

The class `HitsResource` listens to the URL `http://[localhost:8080]/x-ray/resources/hits`. The first part, which is inside the square brackets, is the server's IP address and port. x-ray is the name of the WAR file. The context path can be configured only in a standard way with an EAR file only (see Listing 29).

```
<application version="6" xmlns="http://java.sun.com/xml/ns/javaee"
xmlns:xsi="http://www.w3.org/2001/XMLSchema-instance"
xsi:schemaLocation="http://java.sun.com/xml/ns/javaee http://
java.sun.com/xml/ns/javaee/application_6.xsd">

    <display-name>x-ray</display-name>

    <module>

      <web>

        <web-uri>x-ray-war.war</web-uri>

        <context-root>x-ray-war</context-root>

      </web>

    </module>

    <module>

      <ejb>x-ray-ejb.jar</ejb>

    </module>

</application>
```

Listing 29: Context URL Configuration in an EAR File

The application server usually derives the context URL from the WAR file name. For a custom configuration of the context URI in a standalone WAR file, an application server-specific deployment descriptor or configuration is needed. It is impossible to customize the context URL with a plain WAR file in a server-independent way.

```
@Path("hits")
@Stateless
@Interceptors(PerformanceAuditor.class)
public class HitsResource {

    @Inject
```

60

```
    URLPathExtractor extractor;

    @EJB

    Hits hits;


    @PUT

    @Consumes({MediaType.TEXT_PLAIN})

    public Response updateStatistics(@Context HttpHeaders httpHeaders,
String url) {

        if (!isEmpty(url)) {

    MultivaluedMap<String, String> headers =
httpHeaders.getRequestHeaders();

    Map<String, String> headerMap = new HashMap<String, String>();

    for (Map.Entry<String, List<String>> headerEntries :
headers.entrySet()) {

                String headerName = headerEntries.getKey();

                List<String> headerValuesList = headerEntries.getValue
();

    if (headerValuesList != null && !headerValuesList.isEmpty()) {

                    String headerValue = headerValuesList.get(0);

                    headerMap.put(headerName, headerValue);

                }

            }

            processURL(url, headerMap);

        }

        return Response.noContent().build();

    }


  void processURL(String url, Map<String, String> headerMap) {

        String uniqueAction = extractor.extractPathSegmentFromURL
(url);

        String referer = extractor.extractReferer(url);

        hits.updateStatistics(uniqueAction, referer, headerMap);

    }
```

```
boolean isEmpty(String url) {
    if (url == null) {
        return true;
    }
    String trimmed = url.trim();
    return trimmed.isEmpty();
}


@GET
@Produces({MediaType.TEXT_PLAIN})
public String totalHitsAsString() {
    return hits.totalHitsAsString();
}
}
```

Listing 30: HitsResource—The Server-Side Skeleton

The method `updateStatistics` in the `HitsResource` stateless session bean is annotated with the `@PUT` and `@Consumes({MediaType.TEXT_PLAIN})` annotations. All PUT requests will, therefore, be routed to the `updateStatistics` method.

The content of the `@Consumes` annotation specifies how to interpret the parameter. It is a plain string. The `MediaType.TEXT_PLAIN` attribute configures a pass-through of the content without any further transformation or interpretation. The string parameter is the result of the encoding of a URI.

The method `processURL` extracts the referer and invokes the business logic.

Also interesting is the return type of the `updateStatistics` method. The `Response` class comes with JAX-RS and simplifies the creation of HTTP codes. `Response` can be conveniently created with a Builder pattern. We are creating a `noContent()` response, which is translated into the HTTP code 204. This HTTP code is returned regardless of the actual process result, even if exceptions exist. A good PUT implementation would return HTTP Created (code 201) in the case of an invocation with a not-yet-existing URI, and it would return HTTP OK (code 200) in the case of an update of already-existing information.

The `updateStatistics` use case is an exception to the rule that a good PUT statement should return code 201 or 200. The x-ray probe is not interested in a feedback, status, or possible errors. Also tracking the distinction between the HTTP codes Created and OK would only

62

introduce additional complexity and processing overhead without adding any additional value. Exceptions and errors couldn't be properly handled and would affect the performance of the application. The x-ray probe forwards as fast as possible to the backend the URI with the corresponding metadata. Exceptions are just ignored regardless of their origin.

The naming of the class `HitsResource` seems strange, but it fits a common REST naming scheme. The plural "Hits" indicates that this class represents a set of resources, not a single resource. Classes responsible for the creation and removal of entities are given a plural name. Updates, detailed information, or further navigation are handled by classes that are given a singular name. We do not have a `HitResource` class, because we do not have a use case for detailed information or updates. In more complex scenarios, it is very common to interchange plurals and singulars by introducing sub-resources.

The last part of the name ("Resource") is independent from the first part. It is only used to separate the REST-related classes from the actual implementation of the business logic. Using "Resource" as a suffix is convenient, because it prevents name clashes. Furthermore, it helps to keep the business logic protocol implementation agnostic.

The method `totalHitsAsString` listens to all GET requests and returns the current number of hits. Such REST behavior is rather unusual for `HitsResource`. You would usually return all hits as JSON or XML containing the URIs for a GET request. In subsequent requests, further information about particular hits would be returned using the previously specified URI. We are returning the computed total number of all hits instead of just returning links to all known hits.

Convenient Transactions

Do we really need transactions? This question is hard to answer; rephrasing it to "Do we really need ACID (atomicity, consistency, isolation, durability)?" makes answering the question easier.

Even for consistent reading from the database, transactions are necessary. Without a transaction, there are also no isolation guarantees (the "I" in "ACID"). And without any isolation guarantees, you could read uncommitted changes and base your assumptions on inconsistent data.

Transaction bookkeeping doesn't impose a huge overhead on overall performance; in fact, the overhead is hardly measurable. An empty, but transactional, EJB method has nearly the same performance as a method denoted with `TransactionAttributeType.NOT_SUPPORTED`. It is always a good approach to access a transactional data source in an active transaction context. Premature optimization is the root of all evil...

Note that the `HitsResource` is an interfaceless stateless session bean (see Listing 30). The lack of any transaction-related annotation implies the `TransactionAttribute(REQUIRED)` setting. `TransactionAttributeType.REQUIRED` means that if there is no existing transaction, a new one will be started. Existing transactions (which are impossible for a REST request) will be reused. A transaction is started before the actual method and committed or rolled back after that. The transactional aspect is a part of the EJB 3.1 specification and it not available in Java EE 6 for other components such as CDI beans. All `HitsResource` methods are already executed inside a transaction context, which is propagated to all participating objects or beans.

`HitsResource` is the boundary of the x-ray backend. It is directly exposed to external clients. Although no transactional resources are accessed inside `HitsResource`, it is convenient to start a transaction at a boundary. The transaction is propagated to all participants invoked inside a method.

Transparent transaction propagation is one of the most elegant design decisions in Java EE 6. To achieve this behavior, you don't have to configure anything. Not even a single annotation is required to start and propagate a transaction transparently. It is sufficient to introduce the facade as an EJB 3.1 bean. Injected EJB beans, resources, CDI managed beans, and POJOs will all be executed in the same transaction context as the facade.

EJB beans also allow you to transparently introduce additional layers on demand. You can let the complexity of a boundary (a.k.a. facade) grow until it becomes incohesive, too complex, or just hard to test. Then, you can factor out cohesive pieces of functionality into new classes and inject them into the facade. The facade becomes leaner and the extracted classes become independently testable. Because of EJB 3.1, the process of refactoring has no impact on consistency. It doesn't make any difference whether several transaction participants are accessed inside the transaction initiating class or injected beans. The participating components only have to be executed in the same thread and transaction.

In accordance with the approach described here, incohesive business logic was extracted from the boundary and put into newly created layers behind it. It is also a common pattern to extract the facade functionality from an existing boundary and degrade the boundary into a "usual" class. This was also done during x-ray development.

In my first proof of concept, the `Hits` class implemented the actual business logic as well as REST functionality. In subsequent iterations, I created a new `@Stateless` EJB bean `HitsResource`. The motivation behind this factoring was the principle of Separation of Concerns. Before the refactoring, the `Hits` bean was responsible for cross-cutting concerns such as transactions, threading, exposure of REST services, and the actual implementation of the business logic. Such an approach saves some code, but it makes the business logic dependent on the concrete implementation of the protocol that is used (REST, in this case), so the business logic is unusable in another context.

Consider the method `updateStatistics` (see Listing 31). Using `javax.ws.rs.core.Response` as a return value doesn't make any sense in the context of JavaServer Faces (JSF), Servlets, or SOAP, or even in the context of other EJB beans.

```
@PUT

@Consumes({MediaType.TEXT_PLAIN})

public Response updateStatistics(String url) {

    //...

    return Response.noContent().build();

}
```

Listing 31: An Example of a Method Dependent on JAX-RS

JAX-RS injection of, for example, `UriInfo`, is even more destructive:

```
import javax.ws.rs.core.UriInfo;

import javax.ws.rs.core.Context;

@Context UriInfo info;
```

The injection would work only in the case of a REST invocation. Any use in another context would lead to `NullPointerException` caused by a not-injected `@Context UriInfo info`.

The separation of REST and business logic with the introduction of Resource classes is straightforward. You only have to introduce the new boundaries (or resources) as EJB 3.1 beans. Without configuring anything, the first layer will always start the transaction, which gets transparently propagated to all invoked participants.

EJB and POJO Injection

Two dependent classes are injected into the `HitsResource` boundary—the class `URLPathExtractor` and the EJB 3.1 bean `Hits`.

`URLPathExtractor` is just a utility class without any dependency on Java EE 6. It is injected with the `@Inject` annotation. The only requirement is the existence of a default constructor.

I factored out `URLPathExtractor` from `HitsResource` to mitigate the complexity and increase testability. I did this after few iterations. Designing Java EE applications is very similar to plain old, but pragmatic, Java Platform, Standard Edition (Java SE) design. Introduction of new layers happens on demand in a bottom-up fashion. There is no need for a top-down introduction of architectural artifacts. The old "divide and conquer" algorithm (http://en.wikipedia.org/wiki/Divide_and_conquer_algorithm) can be applied for Java EE 6 as well. Overly bloated and

65

complex classes are divided into cohesive and easier-to-understand pieces after a few iterations. No upfront design is needed, because no upfront overhead exists. From the design perspective, there is absolutely no difference between POJOs, EJB beans, managed beans, or JPA entities.

The `URLPathExtractor` is injected with `@Inject`, and the `Hits` boundary is injected with the `@EJB` annotation. This distinction is not necessary. You could also inject both with `@Inject`. If you do so, you have to keep in mind that `@Inject` injection is more powerful than EJB beans. The support for inheritance is very poor in EJB, but it is very powerful in CDI managed beans. Trying to inject polymorphic EJB beans with `@Inject` could lead to nasty runtime problems.

Eventual Consistency with Singletons

Every click is forwarded to the backend by an HTTP filter and forwarded to `x-ray-services` via HTTP PUT. But how do we persist and compute the statistics? We are actually not interested in tracking user behavior; rather we are interested in the popularity of posts. We could insert new URIs into the database and update the statistics for already existing URIs. On every click, you would have to perform an insert or database update. The database would become a potential bottleneck, and we would have to deal with it from the very first increment. On the other hand, a central database as central data store is the most consistent approach. The system is always in a consistent state at every point in time. So, how do we decide what consistency level is actually needed? The answer is easy. A developer cannot just decide that; it is a business decision.

In the role of domain expert, I'm really interested in the popularity of each post. At the time of this writing, there are about one thousand posts. It would be interesting to know how popular each one is. Such statistics don't have to be consistent in real time. A daily update would be sufficient. Before x-ray, I used weekly Webalizer (http://www.mrunix.net/webalizer/) runs for the computation and published the statistics monthly. A daily statistic update would be a huge improvement compared to the previous situation.

The next interesting statistic is currently trending topics. It is interesting to see what happens in real time, but these results don't have to be stored persistently. They could get lost at every server restart or crash. Persisting the current trend would be a nice, but not an absolutely necessary, feature. Furthermore, it turns out that so far, the Linux, JDK 1.6, GlassFish, and Hypersonic database (HSQLDB) (http://hsqldb.org) combination is extremely stable. The server has never crashed thus far. It ran for months, even years. I restarted it only for updates. Such considerations are also valuable in commercial projects. High availability and extreme consistency are overrated in the real world. Clients prescribe 24/7 availability for noncritical software without even thinking about the consequences.

It would also be nice to have the total number of daily hits and hits from the previous day.

This statistic also doesn't have to be persistent. Upon server crash or restart, the daily hits counter could just be reset.

Beyond that, I would be also interested in the referers statistics, especially the information about who (for example, the user agent) visits my blog and from where (referer) the visitor is coming. Sometimes, my server has to handle serious load peaks, and it hard to say what caused the load. With the extraction and computation of referer statistics, I would at least know whether dzone.com, digg, hackernews, or javalobby caused the traffic or whether it was an attempted Denial of Service attack.

The x-ray functional and non-functional requirements are already unusually precise. In the real world, expectations regarding the consistency and persistence are usually higher during the first iterations. To satisfy the high non-functional requirements, we probably have to start with the implementation of JPA 2 persistence and perform some stress tests afterwards. JPA 2 integrates very nicely with EJB 3.1 and CDI, so this won't cause additional overhead.

Knowing the use cases and being able to loosen the consistency and availability requirements sparks another idea: the introduction of a cache for the computation of statistics with deferred writes to persistent storage. With EJB 3.1 and Java EE 6 such a cache is very easy to implement…

Singletons Are Not Completely Dead

Avoiding `@Singleton` beans for the implementation of business logic is a good idea. `@Stateless`, and sometimes `@Stateful` session beans and CDI managed beans, is more suitable for this purpose.

`@Singleton` beans came with EJB 3.1 in Java EE 6 and caught lots of interest. The container creates a single `@Singleton` bean per JVM instance. On one server, you get exactly one instance. If your server is running in a clustered environment, the application server creates an instance for each node (JVM). Java EE 6 singletons are similar to the Java SE Singleton (anti) pattern. They are, however, subtle differences between the two.

In Java EE, you can get more than one singleton instance in a cluster. In Java SE, you can get multiple singleton instances by loading them by multiple class loaders. The real problem is not the number of instances; rather it is the concurrency behavior. Java SE singletons can be accessed by multiple threads, which is fast, but not necessarily consistent. A `@Singleton` EJB can be accessed only by one thread a time, so it will be always consistent. This consistency comes with a high price—the `@Singleton` annotation without any further configuration causes serial execution of threads and becomes a bottleneck.

This is the default configuration of a singleton, but you can very easily override it. Convention over Configuration in the context of a singleton means serial execution, but this behavior can be changed with a single annotation.

The `@ConcurrencyManagement(ConcurrencyManagementType.BEAN)` annotation makes the `@Singleton` very fast, but inconsistent. With the annotation `ConcurrencyManagement.BEAN`, the EJB container does not care about serializing the access and the singleton becomes accessible by multiple threads. Several threads are able to access and modify a global data structure without any synchronization, which causes eventual inconsistencies.

Fortunately, JDK 1.5 brought us lock-free, but still consistent, collections. The `java.util.concurrent.ConcurrentHashMap` is a lock-free but consistent `Map` and it meets our requirements perfectly. A `ConcurrentHashMap` can be directly exposed in a `@Singleton` to multiple threads without any synchronization (see Listing 32):

```
@Singleton

@ConcurrencyManagement(ConcurrencyManagementType.BEAN)

public class Hits {


private ConcurrentHashMap<String, AtomicLong> hits = null;


@PostConstruct

public void preloadCache() {

hits = new ConcurrentHashMap<String, AtomicLong>(hits);

//...preloading

}
```
Listing 32: Using ConcurrentHashMap as a Cache

A method in a `@Singleton` annotated with `@PostConstruct` will be invoked just after the creation of the instance and the injection of all dependencies. You can rely on the existence of all injected fields. Either the injection is successful, or the instance will not be created.

We are using the `ConcurrentHashMap` as a cache. The `ConcurrentHashMap` is initialized in the `@PostConstruct preloadCache` method just to group the whole initialization process of the class in one place. Just after the initialization, the cache gets prepopulated from the persistent store at startup.

The method `updateStatistics` is directly invoked by the `HitsResource`, which is the REST boundary (see Listing 33).

```
    public void updateStatistics(String uri, String referer,
Map<String, String> headerMap) {

        try {

            if (urlFilter.ignore(uri) || httpHeaderFilter.ignore
(headerMap)) {

                numberOfRejectedRequests.incrementAndGet();

                return;

            }

            storeURI(uri);

            if (referer != null && !referer.isEmpty()) {

                storeReferer(referer);

            }

        } catch (Exception e) { // logging…

        }

    }
```

Listing 33: Protocol-Agnostic Boundary Implementation

The implementation is straightforward. It is a simple facade that invokes the `storeURI` and `storeReferer` after checking the preconditions. The `storeURI` invokes two other methods:

```
    void storeURI(String uniqueAction) {

        storeHitStatistics(uniqueAction);

        if (isRelevantForTrend(uniqueAction)) {

            storeTrending(uniqueAction);

        }

    }
```

Inside the `storeHitsStatistics` method, the actual magic happens. The `putIfAbsent` method is the reason for using `ConcurrentHashMap`, instead of the usual `Map` interface, in the declaration:

```
    long storeHitStatistics(String uniqueAction) {

        hitStatistics.putIfAbsent(uniqueAction, new AtomicLong());

        AtomicLong hitCount = hitStatistics.get(uniqueAction);

        return hitCount.incrementAndGet();
```

```
}
```

For an unknown URI, a new `AtomicLong` instance is created. If the URI already exists, the corresponding `AtomicInteger` instance is returned and its value is increased with `incrementAndGet`. Also, the `AtomicInteger` is working in an optimistic and consistent manner without blocking. It uses the "compare and set/swap" algorithm (http://en.wikipedia.org/wiki/Compare-and-swap) behind the scenes. The principle is similar to optimistic locks in JPA.

In JPA, the value of the field marked with the `@Version` annotation is remembered and compared during the update phase. An unchanged value indicates a consistent state, because there were no modifications by other threads or transactions in the database. If the cached value (the "before" image) and the actual value in the data store do not match, an exception is thrown. With JPA, an `OptimisticLockException` is thrown. The `AtomicLong` implementation, on the other hand, relies on native code and is able to update the value automatically at the CPU level.

A single roundtrip ends with the updating of the statistics stored in the `ConcurrentHashMap`. The updates do not lock the data structure, so the performance of the method `updateStatistics` is dependent only on the scalability of the `ConcurrentHashMap`. With a simple `@Singleton`, we managed to implement a consistent, lock-free, and very scalable data store. The only thing we are missing is failure tolerance and persistence.

@Asynchronous or Not

It turns out, that the performance of the `updateStatistics` method is not even measurable. This is a shame, because this method is the perfect example for the `@Asynchronous` annotation. To make it execute asynchronously in an application server thread pool, the method `updateStatistics` has to be annotated with the `@Asynchronous` annotation:

```
@Asynchronous
public void updateStatistics(String uri, String referer) {

}
```

The asynchronous method invocation decouples the execution of this method from its invoker. Then, the client doesn't have to wait until the method returns.

The method `updateStatistics` is executed in a background thread managed by an application server. Because it is an EJB bean, the invocation is transactional by default. Convention over Configuration does not play very well with transactions and asynchronous method execution. In the default case, the transaction gets propagated and the asynchronous method is executed in the caller's transaction. More appropriate for asynchronous invocation is the `RequiresNew` transaction level:

```
@Asynchronous
@TransactionAttribute(TransactionAttributeType.REQUIRES_NEW)
public void updateStatistics(String uri, String referer) {

//...

}
```

So far, the whole implementation has been realized without locking. No complex algorithms or slow IO operations are involved. The whole transaction is executed in one process, so there is no need for XA or two-phase commit (2PC) semantics. As already noted, the execution of the method `updateStatistics` is hardly measurable through Java means. Although the method signature and its functionality would perfectly fit the paradigm of `@Asynchronous` invocation, using `@Asynchronous` invocation would cause additional overhead. Each request would be passed to a thread pool and executed in a separate thread. The duration of the `updateStatistics` method was not measurable, so the asynchronous processing would be processed almost synchronously. Asynchronous invocation of a very fast method causes additional resource overhead without any benefit.

An interesting question to ask is: "What happens in the worst case?" Let's assume that for some reason, our back-end implementation will block every request forever. In this case, the previously discussed client-side thread pool in the x-ray probe would reject incoming requests. The statistics for the incoming requests would be lost, but the user wouldn't notice that. Such behavior is perfectly viable in our case. A good user experience has priority over exact statistics.

Let's assume the same scenario (blocking method call) for an asynchronous EJB method on the server side. Each new request would lock an additional bean instance and allocate a thread from the pool. More and more fresh bean instances would be locked until the pool was empty. After the exhaustion of all pool resources, the client would be blocked. This scenario is, however, properly handled in our case.

An asynchronous invocation would decouple the client but bind more threads and consume more resources. Without a thread pool with a bounded size, acquiring a new thread for each new, but slow, request could lead to `OutOfMemoryException`.

In our case, the implementation of the safety valve is better located on the client side. We can even shut down the `x-ray-services` application without impacting stability or even the performance of the client (that is, the blog).

Persistence for Availability

The x-ray backend stores its state in key-value pairs. Also, simple statistics, such as the computation of total hits, are performed on the key-value store. The state of the transient cache is flushed into a persistent store in a configurable period repeatedly. A crash or reboot between the synchronization points would lead to data loss. The shorter the period between flushes, the less data gets lost.

I implemented the periodic synchronization with the `@Singleton Hits` EJB bean and the `@Schedule` annotation (see Listing 34).

```
@Startup

@Singleton

@ConcurrencyManagement(ConcurrencyManagementType.BEAN)

@Interceptors(PerformanceAuditor.class)

public class Hits {


    @EJB

    PersistentHitStore hitStore;

    @EJB

    PersistentRefererStore refererStore;


    //...
    private ConcurrentHashMap<String, AtomicLong> hitStatistics =
null;
    private ConcurrentHashMap<String, AtomicLong> trending = null;
    private ConcurrentHashMap<String, AtomicLong> refererStatistics =
null;


    @PostConstruct

    public void preloadCache() {

        Map<String, AtomicLong> hits = hitStore.getHits();

        Map<String, AtomicLong> referers = refererStore.getReferers();

        hitStatistics = new ConcurrentHashMap<String, AtomicLong>
```

```
(hits);

        trending = new ConcurrentHashMap<String, AtomicLong>();

        refererStatistics = new ConcurrentHashMap<String, AtomicLong>
(referers);

    }


    public void updateStatistics(String uri, String referer,
Map<String, String> headerMap) {

            //...

    }


    @Schedule(minute = "*/5", hour = "*", persistent = false)

    public void persistHitsCache() {

        hitStore.store(hitStatistics);

    }


    @Schedule(minute = "*/5", hour = "*", persistent = false)

    public void persistReferersCache() {

        refererStore.store(refererStatistics);

    }


    @Schedule(hour = "*/1", persistent = false)

    public void resetTrends() {

        trending.clear();

    }

    //...methods ommitted

}
```

Listing 34: Eventual Persistency with @Schedule

Every five minutes (minute = "*/5"), the method persistHitsCache is invoked in a transaction context by the container. In subsequent iterations, I factored out the periodic execution into a dedicated class (see Listing 35) and made the period's length configurable.

```
    @Singleton
```

```
@Startup
public class HitsFlushTimer {

    @Inject
    private int hitsFlushRate;

    @EJB
    Hits hits;

    @Resource
    TimerService timerService;

    @PostConstruct
    public void initializeTimer() {
      ScheduleExpression expression = new ScheduleExpression();
      expression.minute("*/" + this.hitsFlushRate).hour("*");
      TimerConfig timerConfig = new TimerConfig();
      timerConfig.setPersistent(false);
      timerService.createCalendarTimer(expression, timerConfig);
    }

    @Timeout
    public void initiateFlush() {
        this.hits.persistHitsCache();
    }
}
```

Listing 35: Configurable Scheduler

On every "timeout," the cache, which is implemented as a `ConcurrentHashMap`, is passed to the `PersistentHitStore` control. Because hits and referrers are processed in exactly the same way, the common logic was factored out into an abstract `PersistentStore` class (see Listing 36):

```java
public abstract class PersistentStore {


  public void store(Map<String,AtomicLong> cache){
      Set<Entry<String, AtomicLong>> entrySet = cache.entrySet();
        for (Entry<String, AtomicLong> entry : entrySet) {
            String id = entry.getKey();
            AtomicLong hitCount = entry.getValue();
            updateStatistics(id,hitCount);

        }

    }

  abstract void updateStatistics(String id, AtomicLong hitCount);

}
```

Listing 36: Template Pattern for Reuse of Iteration Logic

`PersistentStore` is an implementation of the Gang of Four's Template pattern (http://en.wikipedia.org/wiki/Template_pattern). The interesting information is extracted from the `Map` and an abstract method `updateStatistics` is invoked with the extracted information (see Listing 37):

```java
@Stateless
@Interceptors(PerformanceAuditor.class)
public class PersistentHitStore extends PersistentStore{


    @PersistenceContext(unitName="hitscounter")
    EntityManager em;


    @Override
    public void updateStatistics(String id, AtomicLong hitCount) {
        Hit hit = getManaged(id);
        hit.setCount(hitCount.get());
```

```
    }

    public Hit getManaged(String id){
        Hit found = em.find(Hit.class, id);
        if(found == null){
            found = new Hit(id,0);
            found = em.merge(found);
        }
        return found;
    }

    //...

}
```

Listing 37: Persisting the Transient Cache with JPA

The class `PersistentHitStore` from Listing 37 implements the abstract method `updateStatistics` and is responsible for storing the `Hit` entity in a relational database using JPA. The overridden method `updateStatistics` fetches a managed `Hit` entity and overwrites its hit count. Because `updateStatistics` is already invoked in a transaction started in the `Hits` boundary, all changed entities will be transparently updated at commit time. No further `EntityManager#merge` invocations are required to update already managed entities.

The method `getManaged` tries to fetch the `Hit` entity with a URI (the primary key). Either an already existing entity will be returned or a new entity will be created and merged (that is, attached). It is important to note that the `javax.persistence.EntityManager#merge` method returns an already attached instance, but the parameter itself becomes not managed after the invocation.

When @Asynchronous Becomes Dangerous

The method `store` (see Listing 36) is `void` and would be a perfect candidate for the "fire and forget" communication style. Although the method `store` is a perfect candidate for background processing, I did not annotate it with `@Asynchronous`. The reason for the synchronous invocation is the indirect execution by a timer (`@Schedule`):

```
@Schedule(minute = "*/5", hour = "*", persistent = false)
public void persistHitsCache() {
    hitStore.store(hitStatistics);
```

```
}
```

A synchronous `store` method blocks the timer and delays its next invocation. The synchronous execution prevents launching the `persistHitsCache` method asynchronously and concurrently by timers. Preventing uncontrolled growth of asynchronous invocations is crucial for the stability of the system. Every asynchronous invocation requires a free thread, which in turn binds memory. Uncontrolled thread creation causes `OutOfMemoryError`, so the thread pool responsible for handling `@Asynchronous` methods would have been bounded anyway.

Overabundant threads caused by timer executions of the slow, but asynchronous, `store` method is theoretically a possibility, but this would occur only if the `store` method takes longer than the scheduled time. In the current setup, x-ray persists every 60 seconds. The slowest invocation ever of the method `store` took 600 ms and the average is about 10 ms.

Who Reads Logs—Or How to Monitor Your Application

Logging is ubiquitous. We don't even question whether to write logs anymore; instead, we debate how to write them. The discussion usually starts with choosing built-in `java.util.logging`, Simple Logging Facade for Java (SLFJ) (http://www.slf4j.org/), or Commons Logging (http://commons.apache.org/logging/) libraries.

A more interesting question is not how to write logs, but what information a log should include. It is also useful to know who actually will read the log files and how the log files can be accessed. Sometimes, it might be difficult, or even impossible, to access a file system on the production machine. In this case, log files become worthless for debugging purposes.

In the x-ray case, I'm also in the "operations" role so I can freely choose what will be written to log files, how it will be written, and when it will be written. Writing logs for debugging purposes is not important, because I'm able to remotely debug the application any time.

More interesting is the performance behavior in the production environment. I was curious how slow, simple, and unoptimized code is and whether there was any need for action. Systematic performance measurements are accomplished by an EJB 3 interceptor. `PerformanceAuditor` measures the performance and logs exceptions of all invoked methods (see Listing 38).

```
public class PerformanceAuditor {

    private static final Logger LOG = Logger.getLogger
(PerformanceAuditor.class.getName());


    @AroundTimeout

    @AroundInvoke
```

```
public Object measurePerformance(InvocationContext context) throws
Exception{

        String methodName = context.getMethod().toString();

        long start = System.currentTimeMillis();

        try{

            return context.proceed();

        }catch(Exception e){

            LOG.log(Level.SEVERE, "!!!During invocation of: {0}
exception occured: {1}", new Object[]{methodName,e});

            throw e;

        }finally{

            LOG.log(Level.INFO, "{0} performed in: {1}", new Object[]
{methodName, (System.currentTimeMillis() - start)});

        }

    }

}
```

Listing 38: Performance Logging Interceptor

All boundaries and services were intercepted and each invocation was logged in the following format:

```
[#|2011-02-16T19:06:00.944+0100|INFO|glassfish3.0.1|
com.abien.xray.business.monitoring.PerformanceAuditor|
_ThreadID=130998;_ThreadName=Thread-1;|public void
com.abien.xray.business.store.boundary.Hits.persistHitsCache()
performed in: 892|#]
```

It worked, but the log files grew in an uncontrolled way, and I had to use a combination of tail and grep commands to filter the interesting information. Most of the method invocations were performed in 0 ms, which made also the majority of the entries less interesting.

I rarely searched the log files and was more interested in the current state of the system. I ran the command tail -f server.log | grep 'performed in:' all the time to get an idea of what the system was actually doing. Log files are misused as a real-time communication medium when no one is interested in historical content.

Instead of writing the entries to disk as strings and then extracting pieces of data with fancy commands, interesting information can be aggregated, preprocessed, and published in real time. With Java Management Extensions (JMX) it is trivial to expose useful management information to an easily accessible management infrastructure, such as VisualVM, as type-safe Java objects.

MXBeans—The Easy Way to Expose Cohesive Data

MXBeans are an easy-to-use extension of the standard MBeans. You only have to use the MXBean ending in the interface instead of MBean (see Listing 39). The name of the realizing class does not have a suffix. Getters are exposed as read-only properties, and setters are needed to make the properties changeable remotely via the JMX agent. Methods appear as buttons in the operation area and can also be invoked remotely.

In the context of x-ray, particularly interesting are the top worst-performing methods.

```
public interface MonitoringResourceMXBean {

    List<Invocation> getSlowestMethods();

    Map<String,String> getDiagnostics();

    String getNumberOfExceptions();

    void clear();

}
```

Listing 39: MXBean Needed for Exposure to JConsole

The slowest methods are exposed with the `List<Invocation> getSlowestMethods()` method. The `Invocation` class is a typical JavaBean with read-only properties (Listing 40).

```
    @XmlRootElement
@XmlAccessorType(XmlAccessType.FIELD)
public class Invocation implements Comparable<Invocation>{

    @XmlAttribute
    private String methodName;

    @XmlAttribute
    private Long invocationPerformance;

    public Invocation(String methodName, long invocationPerformance) {
        this.methodName = methodName;
        this.invocationPerformance = invocationPerformance;
    }


    public Invocation() { /* JAXB...*/}
```

79

```java
    public String getMethodName() {
        return methodName;
    }
    public long getInvocationPerformance() {
        return invocationPerformance;
    }
    public boolean isSlowerThan(Invocation invocation){
        return this.compareTo(invocation) > 0;
    }
    @Override
    public int compareTo(Invocation anotherInvocation){
        return this.invocationPerformance.compareTo
(anotherInvocation.invocationPerformance);
    }
//…equals, hashCode and toString are not included
}
```

Listing 40: JavaBean Exposed via JMX

Only the getters are crucial for the JMX exposure. The Java Architecture for XML Binding (JAXB) annotations (for example, @XmlRootElement) are used only for JSON/XML serialization in JAX-RS and are irrelevant in JMX. The class Invocation is exposed via REST in parallel to JMX. Without MXBeans, the exposure of a Data Transfer Object, such as the Invocation class, to the MBean server would not work. Only unrelated primitive data types can be exposed as an MBean.

MonitoringResourceMXBean is implemented directly by a singleton EJB 3.1 bean (see Listing 41). It turns out that singletons are perfectly suited as an MXBean implementation.

```java
@Singleton
@Startup
@LocalBean
@Path("monitoring")
@ConcurrencyManagement(ConcurrencyManagementType.BEAN)
public class MonitoringResource implements MonitoringResourceMXBean {
    private MBeanServer platformMBeanServer;
```

```java
    private ObjectName objectName = null;

    private ConcurrentHashMap<String,Invocation> methods = new
ConcurrentHashMap<String,Invocation>();

    private ConcurrentHashMap<String,String> diagnostics = new
ConcurrentHashMap<String,String>();

    private AtomicLong exceptionCount;


    @PostConstruct

    public void registerInJMX() {

        this.exceptionCount = new AtomicLong();

        try{

            objectName = new ObjectName
("XRayMonitoring:type="+this.getClass().getName());

            platformMBeanServer =
ManagementFactory.getPlatformMBeanServer();

            platformMBeanServer.registerMBean(this,objectName);

        }catch(Exception e){

            throw new IllegalStateException("Problem during
registration of Monitoring into JMX:" +e);

        }

    }

    @GET

    @Path("exceptionCount")

    @Produces(MediaType.TEXT_PLAIN)

    @Override

    public String getNumberOfExceptions(){

        return String.valueOf(exceptionCount.get());

    }



    @Override

    public Map<String, String> getDiagnostics() {

        return diagnostics;

    }
```

```
    @Override

    @DELETE

    public void clear(){

            methods.clear();

    }

    @PreDestroy

    public void unregisterFromJMX(){

      try{

       platformMBeanServer.unregisterMBean(this.objectName);

      }catch (Exception e){

            throw new IllegalStateException("Problem during
unregistration of Monitoring into JMX:" +e);

      }

    }

//bookkeeping methods omitted

}
```

Listing 41: MX Bean/JAX-RS Monitoring Hybrid

An EJB 3.1 singleton exists only once in a JVM. The `@PostConstruct` method is automatically invoked by `@Startup @Singleton` at startup or deployment time. This behavior solves the MBean registration problem. A JMX bean can be registered only once at the `MBeanServer`. An attempt to register an already registered MBean causes an `javax.management.InstanceAlreadyExistsException`. It is impossible to implement a robust MBean registration with stateless session beans without violating the specification and programming restrictions, in particular. Upon increasing load, the server creates multiple stateless session bean instances. The `@PostConstruct` method is executed once per created instance and the MXBean would be registered multiple times.

The `MonitoringResource` bean (Listing 41) registers itself in the `MBeanServer` at startup (method `registerInJMX` in Listing 41) and unregisters at shutdown in the method `unregisterFromJMX`.

Singleton EJB 3.1 `MonitoringResource` is an active resource, and it doesn't have to be managed by other components. To the contrary, it can be easily injected to other components, for example, interceptors.

`MonitoringResource` was injected to the `PerformanceAuditor` interceptor (see Listing 42), which forwards the method name, measured performance, and any exceptions that occurred.

So, I completely removed logging statements in favor of JMX for performance analytics.

```
public class PerformanceAuditor {

    private static final Logger LOG = Logger.getLogger
(PerformanceAuditor.class.getName());

    @EJB

    MonitoringResource monitoring;


    @AroundTimeout

    @AroundInvoke

    public Object measurePerformance(InvocationContext context) throws
Exception{

        String methodName = context.getMethod().toString();

        long start = System.currentTimeMillis();

        try{

            return context.proceed();

        }catch(Exception e){

            LOG.log(Level.SEVERE, "!!!During invocation of: {0}
exception occured: {1}", new Object[]{methodName,e});

            monitoring.exceptionOccurred(methodName,e);

            throw e;

        }finally{

            long duration = System.currentTimeMillis() - start;

            monitoring.add(methodName,duration);

        }

    }

}
```

Listing 42: Forwarding Data to a JMX Bean

Distributing Events Without JMS—Leaner Than an Observer

PerformanceAuditor is an interceptor and can be applied to EJB beans and managed beans declaratively:

```
@Startup

@Singleton
```

83

```
@ConcurrencyManagement(ConcurrencyManagementType.BEAN)
```
@Interceptors(PerformanceAuditor.class)
```
public class Hits {}
```

The intercepted beans know only the interceptor, not the `MonitorResource`. There is no direct coupling between the business logic and the monitoring cross-cutting aspect. Performance metrics at the method level are useful, but they are not sufficient for detailed monitoring. Every component can produce monitoring data beyond method performance, which might be interesting for JMX exposure. But how can the data be pushed from the business components to `MonitoringResource` without injecting it? Direct coupling between arbitrary business logic and `MonitoringResource` increases the complexity and decreases testability. Furthermore, every EJB bean interested in exposing monitoring data would be dependent on `MonitoringResource`.

Built-in event distribution in the CDI specification elegantly solves this issue. An `Event` instance is injected instead of `MonitoringResource`:

```
@Inject
Event<Diagnostics> monitoring;
```

The class `Diagnostics` simplifies the construction of `java.util.Map` and represents the actual message being distributed (see Listing 43).

```
public class Diagnostics {

        private Map<String,String> parameters = null;

        private Diagnostics(String name,Object value){

        this.parameters = new HashMap<String,String>();

        this.parameters.put(name, String.valueOf(value));

    }

    public static Diagnostics with(String name,Object value){

        return new Diagnostics(name, value);

    }

    public Diagnostics and(String name,Object value){

        this.parameters.put(name, String.valueOf(value));

        return this;

    }

    public Map<String,String> asMap(){

        return this.parameters;
```

```
        }

}
```

Listing 43: Diagnostics: The CDI Message

Apparently, there are no specific requirements for a "CDI message." It can be an arbitrary POJO or even a primitive wrapper type. A CDI message is sent by invoking the `fire` method of the injected `Event` instance:

```
void sendMonitoringData(){

        int hitCacheSize = this.hitStatistics.getCacheSize();

        int hitDirtyEntriesCount =
this.hitStatistics.getDirtyEntriesCount();

        int refererCacheSize = this.refererStatistics.getCacheSize();

        int refererDirtyEntriesCount =
this.refererStatistics.getDirtyEntriesCount();

  Diagnostics diagnostics = Diagnostics.with
("hitCacheSize",hitCacheSize).

  and("hitDirtyEntriesCount",hitDirtyEntriesCount).

  and("refererCacheSize",refererCacheSize).

  and("refererDirtyEntriesCount",refererDirtyEntriesCount).

  and("numberOfRejectedRequests",this.numberOfRejectedRequests);

        monitoring.fire(diagnostics);

  }
```

Therefore, `MonitoringResource` receives the `Diagnostic` instance class without knowing its origin:

```
public void onNewDiagnostics(@Observes Diagnostics diagnostics){

        Map<String,String> map = diagnostics.asMap();

        if(map != null){

                this.diagnostics.putAll(map);

        }

    }
```

The parameter type behind the annotation `@Observes` has to match the type of the sent event. If the types do not match, the message simply disappears. In contrast to dependency injection, an unsatisfied dependency between the fired event and the corresponding listener does

85

not cause errors or deployment problems.

With CDI events, arbitrary data can be sent between business logic and the monitoring component. The actual payload is a `Map<String,String>`, which can be directly exposed to JMX. Merging two `HashMap` instances with `putAll` is a fast enough operation to be performed synchronously.

The `Diagnostic` event could also be delivered easily by annotating the method with the `@Asynchronous` annotation: **@Asynchronous** `public void onNewDiagnostics` (**@Observes** `Diagnostics diagnostics){}`.

REST for Monitoring

The singleton session bean `MonitoringResource` was exposed as an MXBean and can be directly accessed via JMX. It is also a singleton bean and can expose the monitoring data easily via JAX-RS (REST). See Listing 44. Accessing data via HTTP is especially convenient for scripting and terminal access. Tools such as `curl` or `wget` can directly consume the monitoring data.

```
@Singleton

@Startup

@LocalBean

@Path("monitoring")

@ConcurrencyManagement(ConcurrencyManagementType.BEAN)

public class MonitoringResource implements MonitoringResourceMXBean {


    private ConcurrentHashMap<String,Invocation> methods = new
ConcurrentHashMap<String,Invocation>();

    private ConcurrentHashMap<String,String> diagnostics = new
ConcurrentHashMap<String,String>();

    private AtomicLong exceptionCount;


    @GET

    @Produces({MediaType.APPLICATION_JSON,MediaType.APPLICATION_XML})

    public List<Invocation> getSlowestMethods(

            @QueryParam("max") @DefaultValue("50") int maxResult){

        List<Invocation> list = new ArrayList<Invocation>
(methods.values());

        Collections.sort(list);
```

```java
        Collections.reverse(list);
        if(list.size() > maxResult)
            return list.subList(0,maxResult);
        else
            return list;
    }


    @GET
    @Path("exceptionCount")
    @Produces(MediaType.TEXT_PLAIN)
    @Override
    public String getNumberOfExceptions(){
        return String.valueOf(exceptionCount.get());
    }


    @GET
    @Path("diagnostics")
    @Produces(MediaType.TEXT_PLAIN)
    public String getDiagnosticsAsString(){
        return getDiagnostics().toString();
    }


    @GET
    @Path("diagnostics/{key}")
    @Produces(MediaType.TEXT_PLAIN)
    public String getDiagnosticsAsString(@PathParam("key") String key)
{
        return getDiagnostics().get(key);
    }
    @Override
    @DELETE
    public void clear(){
```

```
            methods.clear();

            exceptionCount.set(0);

            diagnostics.clear();

    }

        //REST irrelevant methods omitted

}
```

Listing 44: Exposing Management Data via REST

It is a lot easier for the administrators and operators to access monitoring data via HTTP/REST than via JMX. The `getSlowestMethods` method in Listing 44 returns a list of `Invocation` instances (see Listing 45).

```
@XmlRootElement

@XmlAccessorType(XmlAccessType.FIELD)

public class Invocation implements Comparable<Invocation>{

    @XmlAttribute

    private String methodName;

    @XmlAttribute

    private Long invocationPerformance;


    public Invocation(String methodName, long invocationPerformance) {

        this.methodName = methodName;

        this.invocationPerformance = invocationPerformance;

    }
```

Listing 45: Using JAXB Annotations for XML and JSON Serialization

Class `Invocation` together with JAXB annotations provides sufficient metadata for the JAX-RS implementation Jersey to generate either JSON or XML from the class structure. Even the serialization works with respect to the Convention over Configuration principle. Without any configuration, the names of the XML and JSON tags are directly derived from the class structure. The default values can be overridden at any time with annotations. The output format can be specified with the `Accept` HTTP header.

Here is a `curl` command:

```
curl -H "Accept: application/json" http://localhost:8080/x-ray/
resources/monitoring
```

The `curl` command returns the `Invocation` instances as a JSON string:

```
{"invocation":[{"@methodName":"public java.util.Map
com.abien.xray.business.store.control.PersistentRefererStore.getRefere
rs()","@invocationPerformance":"399"},

{"@methodName":"public void
com.abien.xray.business.store.boundary.Hits.persistReferersCache
()","@invocationPerformance":"305"}, (…)]}
```

Here's a `curl` command that sets the HTTP header to "application/xml":

```
curl -H "Accept: application/xml" http://localhost:5380/x-ray/
resources/monitoring
```

Then it initiates the delivery of a XML document:

```
<?xml version="1.0" encoding="UTF-8" standalone="yes"?>

<invocations>

<invocation methodName="public java.util.Map
com.abien.xray.business.store.control.PersistentRefererStore.getRefere
rs()" invocationPerformance="399"/>

<invocation methodName="public void
com.abien.xray.business.store.boundary.Hits.persistReferersCache()"
invocationPerformance="305"/>

(…)

</invocations>
```

The signature `getSlowestMethods(@QueryParam("max") @DefaultValue("50") int maxResult)` allows the specification of an optional query parameter `max`. The following existing query parameter is automatically converted into an int and passed as parameter:

```
curl -H "Accept: application/xml" http://localhost:5380/x-ray/
resources/monitoring?max=2
```

Also interesting is the following signature from Listing 44:

```
@GET
@Path("diagnostics/{key}")
@Produces(MediaType.TEXT_PLAIN)
public String getDiagnosticsForKey(@PathParam("key") String key){
    return getDiagnostics().get(key);
}
```

In contrast to a `QueryParameter`, the `String` key parameter of the method `getDiagnosticsForKey` is extracted from the last segment of the URL:

```
http://localhost:8080/x-ray/resources/monitoring/diagnostics/
```
hitCacheSize

It is natural and RESTful to use the last segment as an identifier of the addressed resource (object). The URL can be read fluently as "GET diagnostics with the identifier `hitCacheSize`." Consequently, a GET with a full URL without the key (for example, `http://localhost:5380/ x-ray/resources/monitoring/diagnostics`) would return all diagnostics: `{refererDirtyEntriesCount=0, refererCacheSize=26671, hitCacheSize=3196, hitDirtyEntriesCount=0}`.

All diagnostics are returned by the `getDiagnosticsAsString` method:

```
@GET
@Path("diagnostics")
@Produces(MediaType.TEXT_PLAIN)
public String getDiagnosticsAsString(){
    return getDiagnostics().toString();
}
```

Diagnostics can be reset by a DELETE request:

```
curl -X DELETE http://localhost:8080/x-ray/resources/monitoring/
```

A method denoted with `@DELETE` annotation is bound to DELETE HTTP:

```
@Override
@DELETE
public void clear(){
    methods.clear();
    exceptionCount.set(0);
    diagnostics.clear();
}
```

The `clear` method can be invoked via JMX and REST, providing a true "multi-channel" monitoring architecture.

XML over Annotations?

The interception, as well as major parts of the Java EE functionality, could also be configured in XML. You could even configure the whole application with XML and get rid of annotations entirely. Especially "ivory tower" architects love the clear separation of concerns. The code

90

consists of pure business logic and the configuration resides in XML.

However, in practice, the clear separation is not as elegant as it appears on PowerPoint slides. The XML has to refer to the existing code and this cannot be accomplished without duplication. Fully qualified class names have to be included in XML deployment descriptors and configuration files. The required repetition in XML files is *not* DRY (http://en.wikipedia.org/wiki/Don %27t_repeat_yourself) and causes problems the practice. Every structural refactoring has to be performed transactionally; the class name and the corresponding XML file have to be changed at the same time consistently.

Annotations might be not the best choice in theory, but they are extremely productive in practice. Annotations are already associated with the class, method, or field, so DRYness never was an issue. To develop an annotation-driven application, you only need a typical Java IDE without any support for XML refactoring. Even in the unlikely case that your IDE is not capable of refactoring an annotation, in the end, during the compilation, you will notice the problem.

There are also no surprises working with annotations. You can click on an annotation to see what elements are expected. Most of the annotations are well-documented, so you will get inline documentation as well. Furthermore, annotations are type-safe, so misspelling with modern IDEs is nearly impossible. A major drawback of using annotations over XML is the required recompilation for every change. This shortcoming loses its weight if you have a working continuous integration (CI) environment in place. In such a scenario, every commit triggers an entire build and results in a deployable application.

I built x-ray with only the absolutely necessary deployment descriptors: empty `beans.xml` and `persistence.xml`.

Events...And the Type Is Not Enough

The class `Trend` manages a history of minutely and hourly `Hits` and exposes them via REST. Interestingly, `Trend` is not dependent on any other class and just exposes the history via the `trend/hourly` and `trend/minutely` URIs (see Listing 46). `Trend` is also not injected into any other component; however, it is still able to receive minutely and hourly updates.

```
@Path("trend")
@Singleton
@AccessTimeout(2000)
@Produces({MediaType.APPLICATION_JSON, MediaType.APPLICATION_XML})
public class Trend {
```

```java
    private LinkedList<Statistic> hourly = new LinkedList<Statistic>
();

    private LinkedList<Statistic> minutely = new LinkedList<Statistic>
();


    @GET

    @Path("hourly")

    @Lock(LockType.READ)

    public List<Statistic> hourly(@QueryParam("lastHours")
@DefaultValue("24") int hours) {

        int size = hourly.size();

        if (size <= hours) {

            return hourly;

        }

        return hourly.subList(0, hours);

    }


    @GET

    @Path("minutely")

    @Lock(LockType.READ)

    public List<Statistic> minutely(@QueryParam("lastHours")
@DefaultValue("60") int minutes) {

        int size = minutely.size();

        if (size <= minutes) {

            return minutely;

        }

        return minutely.subList(0, minutes);

    }


    @Lock(LockType.WRITE)

    public void onHourlyStatistic(@Observes @HitsPer(HOUR) long
hitPerMinute) {

        hourly.addFirst(new Statistic(hitPerMinute));

    }
```

```
    @Lock(LockType.WRITE)
    public void onMinutelyStatistic(@Observes @HitsPer(MINUTE) long
hitPerMinute) {

        minutely.addFirst(new Statistic(hitPerMinute));

    }

}
```

Listing 46: Hourly and Minutely History of Hits

Statistics are indirectly passed to `onMinutelyStatistic` and `onHourlyStatistic` using the already introduced CDI events. Both methods are expecting a long as a parameter and would receive all events of type long in parallel.

A qualifier is used to distinguish between different logical events of the same type. In the class `Trend`, the qualifier `@HitsPer(HOUR)`, `@HitsPer(MINUTE)` annotates the parameter as well as the injection point of the `Event` class. If both annotations with the included elements match, the event will be delivered; otherwise it will just disappear. With the custom annotation `HitsPer`, the minutely and hourly delivery of the long event can be distinguished in a fluent way (see Listing 47).

```
import static java.lang.annotation.ElementType.FIELD;

import static java.lang.annotation.ElementType.PARAMETER;

import static java.lang.annotation.RetentionPolicy.RUNTIME;

import java.lang.annotation.Retention;

import java.lang.annotation.Target;

import javax.inject.Qualifier;


@Qualifier

@Retention(RUNTIME)

@Target({FIELD, PARAMETER})

public @interface HitsPer {

    Frequency value();

    enum Frequency {

        MINUTE, HOUR

    }

}
```

Listing 47: HitsPer Custom Qualifier

HitsPer is not just a marker annotation. It contains an embedded enum Frequency with the values MINUTE and HOUR. The only element of the HitsPer annotation that has the name value is Frequency. No default value is declared, so a value has to be provided by every declaration. Together with the provided value, the annotation HitsPer is far more readable as @HitsPer(MINUTE), as shown in Listing 48:

```
@Singleton
public class HourlyStatisticsCalculator {


    @Inject
    @HitsPer(HOUR)
    Event<Long> hourlyEvent;


    @Schedule(hour = "*/1", persistent = false)
    public void computeStatistics() {
        //…
hourlyEvent.fire(currentRate);
    }


}


@Singleton
public class MinutelyStatisticsCalculator {

    @Inject
    @HitsPer(MINUTE)
    Event<Long> minutelyEvent;

    @Schedule(minute = "*/1", hour = "*", persistent = false)
    public void computeStatistics() {
            //...

            minutelyEvent.fire(currentRate);
```

```
}

}
```

Listing 48: Qualification of the Event Injection

Both the `Minutely` and `HourlyStatisticCalculator` classes use the `HitsPer` annotation to inject the `Event` instance. Each class is able to send the recently computed statistic to the corresponding channel separately just by choosing the right value of the `HitsPer` qualifier.

CDI events together with custom qualifiers and asynchronous methods are a viable replacement for JMS `javax.jms.Topic` for a local publish/subscribe (pub/sub) implementation.

REST and HTML Serialization

The JAX-RS implementation Jersey (http://jersey.java.net) supports JSON and XML serialization of JAXB annotated objects. Neither JSON nor XML can be directly consumed by a Web browser without further preprocessing. Because of built-in content negotiation, JAX-RS is able to deliver multiple representations of the same data (see Listing 49). The client specifies the anticipated format with the `Accept` header.

```
@Stateless

@Path("mostpopular")

public class MostPopular extends TitleFilter{

    @EJB

    PersistentHitStore hits;

    @GET

    @Produces
({APPLICATION_XHTML_XML,APPLICATION_JSON,APPLICATION_XML})

    public List<Post> totalHitsAsString(@QueryParam("max")
@DefaultValue("10") int max){

        List<Post> mostPopularPosts = new LinkedList<Post>();

        List<Hit> mostPopularPostsWithoutTitle =
hits.getMostPopularPosts(max);

        for (Hit hit : mostPopularPostsWithoutTitle) {

            mostPopularPosts.add(convert(hit));

        }
```

```
        return getPostsWithExistingTitle(mostPopularPosts,max);

    }


    Post convert(Hit hit){

        long count = hit.getCount();

        String uri = hit.getActionId();

        return new Post(uri, count);

    }

}
```

Listing 49: Declaration of Multiple Representations of Post Object

The specified content of the Accept header has to match one of the declared MediaType constants on the corresponding JAX-RS methods, as shown in Listing 49. The following MediaType constants are supported out of the box: APPLICATION_JSON and APPLICATION_XML.

HTML serialization is not supported by Jersey. For the APPLICATION_XHTML_XML, a custom implementation of the interface MessageBodyWriter has to be implemented and annotated with the corresponding MediaType (see Listing 50).

@Provider

@Produces(MediaType.APPLICATION_XHTML_XML)

```
public class PostHtmlWriter implements

        MessageBodyWriter<List<Post>> {

    @Override

    public boolean isWriteable(Class<?> type, Type genericType,
Annotation[] annotations, MediaType mediaType) {

        return (List.class.isAssignableFrom(type));

    }

    @Override

    public long getSize(List<Post> t, Class<?> type, Type genericType,
Annotation[] annotations, MediaType mediaType) {

        String serialized = serialize(t);

        return serialized.length();
```

96

```java
    }

    @Override
    public void writeTo(List<Post> t, Class<?> type, Type genericType,
Annotation[] annotations, MediaType mediaType, MultivaluedMap<String,
Object> httpHeaders, OutputStream entityStream) throws IOException,
WebApplicationException {

        String serialized = serialize(t);

        entityStream.write(serialized.getBytes());

    }

    public String serialize(List<Post> posts){

        StringBuilder result = new StringBuilder();

        result.append("<ol class=\"posts\">");

        for (int i = 0; i < posts.size(); i++) {

            Post post = posts.get(i);

            result.append("<li class=\"post\">");

            result.append(serialize(post));

            result.append("</li>");

            result.append("\n");

        }

        result.append("</ol>");

        return result.toString();

    }


    public String serialize(Post post){

        StringBuilder serialized = new StringBuilder();

        serialized.append("<a class=\"postLink\" href=\"http://
www.adam-bien.com/roller/abien");

        serialized.append(post.getUri());

        serialized.append("\">");

        serialized.append(post.getShortenedTitle(80));

        serialized.append("</a>");

        serialized.append("<div class=\"hits\">");

        serialized.append(post.getNumberOfHits());

        serialized.append("</div>");
```

```
        return serialized.toString();
    }

}
```

Listing 50: Custom HTML Serializer

The serialization itself is straightforward. The `List<Post>` from the `totalHitsAsString` method is passed to the method `writeTo` of the `MessageBodyWriter` implementation as well as the corresponding context, such as the `MediaType`, annotations, `HttpHeader`, and the `OutputStream`. With the available parameters, the list of `Post` instances have to be converted into the desired format serializing the `List<Post>` into the `OutputStream`. In our case, it is an ordered list of posts with links and a hit number. The HTML representation also contains a reference to a CSS class, which makes it skinnable.

Configuration over Convention with Inversion of Control

The principle of Convention over Configuration is applicable to most architectural and infrastructural settings. In the vast majority of cases, there is only one suitable option, so it doesn't have to be testified and repeated in a configuration file. Given a working Continuous Integration environment, a system can be reconfigured on every "commit" (or push) directly in source code or external resources.

From the usability perspective, it is more convenient to keep the various parts of your configuration in a central location. Regardless of whether such parameters are stored directly in source code, in a configuration file, or in a database, a single point of configuration improves the maintainability.

Flushing of the hits and referer caches in x-ray was implemented in the first iteration with `@Schedule` expression:

```
@Schedule(minute = "*/5", hour = "*", persistent = false)
public void persistHitsCache() {
    hitStore.store(hitStatistics.getChangedEntriesAndClear());
}
```

The timeout period was directly hard-coded in the `Hits` class. The `Hits` class also maintained a referer and trend timer—all with hard-coded values. Because the existence of referers and trend values inside a class named `Hits` is not obvious, the configuration becomes harder to maintain. Although the EJB `Hits` bean can be still considered cohesive, information about referers and trends is derived from a request (hit), so this is not the best place to store the timer configuration.

The duration between cache flushes is an interesting tuning option. Long periods for the Hits cache could improve the database performance significantly. The number of affected URIs would not grow significantly; rather, only the value of their hits would increase. On the other hand, longer periods for the referer cache could lead to slower transactions, because it is more likely that the number of records (blog visitors) would also increase. For both cases, the length of the period between flushes is directly related to the availability of the data. In the event of a server crash or restart, all data between cache flushes would be lost.

I factored out the hard-coded values in the @Schedule annotation into standalone classes and converted them to programmatic timers (see Listing 51).

```
@Singleton
@Startup
public class HitsFlushTimer {

    @Inject
    private int hitsFlushRate;

    @EJB
    Hits hits;

    @Resource
    TimerService timerService;

    @PostConstruct
    public void initializeTimer() {
        ScheduleExpression expression = new ScheduleExpression();
        expression.minute("*/" + this.hitsFlushRate).hour("*");
        TimerConfig timerConfig = new TimerConfig();
        timerConfig.setPersistent(false);
        timerService.createCalendarTimer(expression, timerConfig);
    }
```

```
@Timeout

public void initiateFlush() {

    this.hits.persistHitsCache();

}

}
```

Listing 51: Programmatic and Configurable Timer Configuration

HitsFlushTimer in Listing 51 performs the timer configuration in the @PostConstruct hook. All parameters required for the initialization of a programmatically created timer are passed as ScheduleExpression instances to the injected TimerService. In contrast to the use of @Schedule annotation, a programmatically created timer can be reconfigured without any recompilation. With the injected field hitsFlushRate, the timer can even be configured externally. Dependency Injection of primitive types works without any XML or further ceremony. Only a producer method, or even just a plain field with matching type, is required to perform the injection. A naive producer implementation could be like this:

```
@javax.enterprise.inject.Produces

public int getHitsFlushIntervallInMinutes() {          return 1;

}
```

Thankfully, CDI introduces additional meta-information (InjectionPoint in Listing 52) that can be passed to a producer method on demand.

```
@Startup

@Singleton

public class Configuration {

    private Map<String, String> configuration;

    @PostConstruct

    public void fetchConfiguration() {

        this.configuration = new HashMap<String, String>() {{

            put("version", "0.5");

            put("hitsFlushRate", "1");

            put("referersFlushRate", "1");

        }};

    }

    @javax.enterprise.inject.Produces
```

```java
public String getString(InjectionPoint point) {
    String fieldName = point.getMember().getName();
    return configuration.get(fieldName);
}


@javax.enterprise.inject.Produces
public long getLong(InjectionPoint point) {
    String stringValue = getString(point);
    return Long.parseLong(stringValue);
}


@javax.enterprise.inject.Produces
public int getInteger(InjectionPoint point) {
    String stringValue = getString(point);
    return Integer.parseInt(stringValue);
}


}
```

Listing 52: A Generic Configuration Source

Using a slightly modified version of the producer with an `InjectionPoint` parameter, as demonstrated with the method `String getString(InjectionPoint point)` in Listing 52, makes the definition of a custom qualifier obsolete. The `InjectionPoint` parameter wraps the meta-information about the field, setter, or constructor. It is also possible to obtain the name of the field, which can used as a key for the lookup in a `Map`.

The `Configuration` singleton session bean populates the configuration in the `@PostConstruct` method. All values are still hard-coded, but they reside in a central class with a meaningful name. In the `getString` method, the name of the `InjectionPoint` is used to look up the corresponding value in the populated configuration. The remaining getters only convert a string to the desired type.

Easy Extensibility for the Unlikely Case

Sometimes, it might be necessary to load the configuration from external data sources. In general, environment-dependent parameters, such as IP addresses and passwords, should not be hard-coded. Environmental configuration is usually maintained by administrators or operations without having access to the actual code.

With a minor extension, even external data sources can be loaded and merged on demand with the hard-coded defaults:

```
public interface ConfigurationProvider {
    public Map<String,String> getConfiguration();
}
```

Listing 53: Abstract of Implementation for an Arbitrary Configuration Source

In Listing 53, external configuration sources are abstracted with the ConfigurationProvider interface. You only need to make a realization of the interface available in the module and return a Map<String,String> from a configuration source of your choice. All implementations will be automatically discovered and included at startup.

```
@Startup
@Singleton
public class Configuration {


    private Map<String, String> configuration;


    @Inject
    private Instance<ConfigurationProvider> configurationProvider;


    @PostConstruct
    public void fetchConfiguration() {
        this.configuration = new HashMap<String, String>() {{
            put("version", "0.5");
            put("hitsFlushRate", "1");
            put("referersFlushRate", "1");
```

102

```
        }};

        this.unconfiguredFields = new HashSet<String>();


    mergeWithCustomConfiguration();

}


    void mergeWithCustomConfiguration(){
        for (ConfigurationProvider provider : configurationProvider) {
            Map<String, String> customConfiguration =
provider.getConfiguration();

            this.configuration.putAll(customConfiguration);

        }

    }
```

Listing 54: Extension Mechanism for External Configuration Sources

As shown Listing 54, the realization is surprisingly simple. Instead of directly injecting the `ConfigurationInterface`, a `javax.enterprise.inject.Instance` is injected. An `Instance` can be considered as a proxy, which allows you to dynamically obtain all references of the specified bean. `javax.enterprise.inject.Instance` also implements the `java.lang.Iterable` interface, which allows convenient iteration over all discovered `ConfigurationProvider` implementations.

Iteration over all found `ConfigurationProvider` instances and merging the external configuration with internal `Map` happens in the `mergeWithCustomConfiguration()` method. This simple approach is actually an implementation of the Convention over Configuration principle. Essential configuration is hard-coded but can be overridden by shipping `ConfigurationProvider` implementations with the x-ray services WAR file.

RESTful Configuration

An important principle in REST is the unique identification and manipulation of resources. A resource is "something uniquely identifiable" and matches perfectly with the concept of a domain object in Java. A configuration can be considered to be a resource, and JAX-RS can be used to manipulate the entries inside the `Configuration` domain object.

Our configuration implementation consists of flat key-value pairs, so the concept of hyperlinking is not even necessary. The configuration itself could be mapped to the `/configuration/` URI. A GET request to the `/configuration/` URI returns the whole configuration content.

In our case, the hard-coded parameters would look like JSON format:

```
{hitsFlushRate=1, referersFlushRate=1, version=0.5}
```

A GET request to `/configuration/version` returns the value of `0.5` confirmed with the HTTP code 200 (OK). The version entry could be deleted with the HTTP DELETE request and a command such as this:

```
curl -i -X DELETE [http://localhost:8080/x-ray/]resources/
configuration/version
```

A successful DELETE call is confirmed with HTTP code 204 (No Content).

To manage a configuration, there is no need to distinguish between creating a new entry or overwriting an existing one. For such "save or update" semantics, the HTTP PUT method is perfectly suited. It is defined as following:

"The PUT method requests that the enclosed entity be stored under the supplied Request-URI. If the Request-URI refers to an already existing resource, the enclosed entity SHOULD be considered as a modified version of the one residing on the origin server. If the Request-URI does not point to an existing resource, and that URI is capable of being defined as a new resource by the requesting user agent, the origin server can create the resource with that URI. If a new resource is created, the origin server MUST inform the user agent via the 201 (Created) response..." (http://www.w3.org/Protocols/rfc2616/rfc2616-sec9.html).

An entry could be created or updated with the following command:

```
curl -i -H "Content-Type: text/plain" -X PUT -d "duke" http://
localhost:5380/x-ray/resources/configuration/java
```

A PUT request would either create a new entry or update an existing entry. According to the HTTP RFC, a successful creation has to return the following response:

```
HTTP/1.1 201 Created
Location: http://localhost:5380/x-ray/resources/configuration/java
Content-Type: text/plain
```

On the other hand, an update will return only an HTTP 204 (No Content):

```
HTTP/1.1 204 No Content
```

An HTTP 200 (OK) could be also returned with a meaningful payload in the response body.

Fortunately, the class `Configuration` is a singleton EJB 3.1 bean and can be directly

104

exposed via JAX-RS. The REST behavior specified above can be directly realized with the `Configuration` class. It has to be mapped to a URI first, as shown in Listing 55:

```
@Startup

@Singleton

@Path("configuration")

@Produces(TEXT_PLAIN)

public class Configuration {}
```

Listing 55: Mapping a Resource to a URI

The `@Produces` annotation sets the default mime type for all methods inside the class to `String`. Whatever the JAX-RS methods return will be interpreted as a string. A GET [...]/ configuration request would cause the invocation of the following method:

```
@GET

public String getConfiguration() {

    return this.configuration.toString();

}
```

It would also return to the user the whole configuration converted to a string. In our case, the `java.util.Map#toString` method is used to serialize the content of the configuration to a string.

An entry for a given key is fetched using the `@PathParam("key")` with a `@Path` `("{key}")` template in the method `getEntry`:

```
@GET

@Path("{key}")

public String getEntry(@PathParam("key") String key) {

    return configuration.get(key);

}
```

Creating or modifying an entry requires returning different responses for each case. The method `addEntry` returns either an HTTP 204 (No Content, for an update) or an HTTP 201 (Created, for adding a new entry) with an appropriately set location header to the URI of the created element, as shown in Listing 56:

```
@PUT

@Path("{key}")

@Consumes(TEXT_PLAIN)
```

```java
    public Response addEntry(@PathParam("key") String key, String
value, @Context UriInfo uriInfo) {

        Response response = null;

        if(this.configuration.containsKey(key)){

            response = Response.noContent().build();

        }else{

            URI uri = uriInfo.getAbsolutePathBuilder().build(key);

            response= Response.created(uri).build();

        }

        this.configuration.put(key, value);

        return response;

    }
```

Listing 56: Different Response Codes for Create or Update

The method `deleteEntry` uses, very similarly to `getEntry`, the `PathParam` to remove an entry from the `Map` with the given key:

```java
@DELETE

@Path("{key}")

public Response deleteEntry(@PathParam("key") String key) {

    this.configuration.remove(key);

    return Response.noContent().build();

}
```

The producer methods (annotated with `@Produces`) are not denoted with any scope declaration and, therefore, they are executed in scope dependent on their injection points. An unconfigured producer is defaulted to `@Dependent` scope. `RequestScoped` beans could even be reconfigured on every request, and `SessionScoped` beans could be reconfigured on each new session. With JAX-RS and CDI, it is even possible to reconfigure parts of the system at runtime.

Logger Injection

A centralized configuration should also contain log settings. In general, the logging configuration is externalized into a standalone file. In the x-ray case, the most interesting information is already published to JMX. The log files are used only to track possible problems, but they are disabled in production mode. With the inclusion of logging settings into the already

106

described `Configuration`, maintainability could even be further increased.

To meet the requirement, all `Logger` instances are going to be injected. With injection, you can swap a logger implementation without changing the client code. Different log implementations are created dependent on the configuration. For debug mode, a real `Logger` instance is injected; otherwise, a `DevNullLogger` implementation is used (see Listing 57).

```java
public class LoggerProducer {

    @Inject
    private boolean debug;


    @Produces
    public XRayLogger getLogger(InjectionPoint ip){
        if(debug){
            Class<?> aClass = ip.getMember().getDeclaringClass();
            Logger logger = Logger.getLogger(aClass.getName());
            return new DelegatingLogger(logger);
        }else{
            return new DevNullLogger();
        }
    }

}
```

Listing 57: Configuration-Dependent LoggerProducer

The class `LoggerProducer` in Listing 57 creates `java.util.Logging` wrappers abstracted with a common `XRayLogger` interface (see Listing 58).

```java
public interface XRayLogger {
    public void log(Level level, String message, Object[] par);
    public Logger getLogger();


}
```

Listing 58: Logger Abstraction

The `DelegatingLogger` realization expects a `Logger` instance and delegates all invocations to it (see Listing 59).

```java
public class DelegatingLogger implements XRayLogger{
```

```java
    private Logger logger;

    public DelegatingLogger(Logger logger) {
        this.logger = logger;
    }

    public void log(Level level, String message, Object[] params){
            this.logger.log(level, message, params);
    }

    public Logger getLogger() {
        return logger;
    }
}
```

Listing 59: java.util.Logging Wrapper

DelegatingLogger is the "debugging" setup where all log messages are actually passed to the real log system. In production, a "/dev/null" implementation of the Logger implementation is used (see Listing 60).

```java
@Alternative
public class DevNullLogger implements XRayLogger{
    @Override
    public void log(Level INFO, String string, Object[] object) {
        //ignore everything
    }

    @Override
    public Logger getLogger() {
        return null;
    }
}
```

Listing 60: Null-Object Implementation of XRayLogger

108

DevNullLogger is denoted with the @Alternative annotation and so it is disabled. The @Alternative annotation forces the container to use the LoggerProducer to create the instances, instead of using the default constructor directly. A removal of the @Alternative annotation from DevNullLogger would introduce an ambiguity and would cause deployment errors.

A potential advantage of wrapping the java.util.Logger with a delegate is increased encapsulation. X-ray application code is no longer dependent on java.util.Logger; it is dependent only on the XRayLogger interface. This positive side-effect was not the main goal behind the introduction of the delegate; rather, it was the consequence of central and convenient configuration. It is actually very unlikely that the java.util.Logging framework will be replaced in the near future with an alternative.

The choice regarding the implementation is made in the LoggerProducer class with the injected debug field (see Listing 57). In the default case, DevNullLogger gets instantiated. In debug mode, DelegatingLogger gets instantiated. The value of the debug field is produced by the Configuration singleton session bean.

Unit Test Is Not Integration Test

It is a common misconception that a unit test should always run conveniently in an embedded container and behave like the production system. In fact, the opposite is true: A good unit test should validate the functionality independently of its infrastructure and be as independent as possible from a container. All dependencies should be mocked out, and the behavior of the class under test should be tested in isolation. Mocking out external dependencies with the right framework (for example, by using Mockito (http://mockito.org) is easy and extremely productive. The productivity gains of mocking out the infrastructure are noticeable even in trivial cases and become even more substantial for more complex business logic.

The JUnit (http://junit.org/) test framework can be misused to intentionally implement integration tests. You can launch the JPA environment outside the container and inject the EntityManager to the class under test (CUT) by yourself (see Listing 61).

```
public class UserAgentStatisticsIT {
    private EntityManager em;
    private EntityTransaction tx;
    UserAgentStatistics cut;

    @Before
    public void initializeCUT(){
```

```
        EntityManagerFactory emf =
Persistence.createEntityManagerFactory("integration");

        em = emf.createEntityManager();

        tx = em.getTransaction();

        this.cut = new UserAgentStatistics();

        this.cut.em = em;

    }

}
```

Listing 61: Unit Test with "Real" EntityManager

This, however, isn't a true unit test anymore and should be strictly separated from pure unit tests. Clean separation between unit and integration tests also allows implementation of several build jobs. Unit tests are orders of magnitude faster and will be executed first, and integration tests are slower and executed afterwards. You get instantaneous feedback about the correctness of the business logic and you do not have to wait until all integration tests are passed.

Infrastructure tests are less common, but they are highly recommended in the case of x-ray as well. It doesn't make any sense to mock out the infrastructure to test the x-ray Configuration or LoggerProducer functionality. For both classes, the interaction between the business code (for example, null checks and searching for external configuration providers) and the infrastructure (for example, dependency injection, events, and interception) is particularly interesting. The functionality of both Configuration and LoggerProducer relies entirely on CDI. Mocking out the infrastructure and, thus, CDI would make any sensible testing impossible. It is also important to note that the domain of both classes is a cross-cutting concern that is based on the Java EE 6 infrastructure. The implementation of such infrastructure in a healthy business/enterprise project constitutes only a fraction of the overall code. The vast majority of all unit tests do validate the business logic and only a fraction should require a running container to perform unit tests.

Injection and Infrastructure Testing with Aliens

EJB 3.1 beans, managed beans, or JPA entities are easy to unit test. They are nothing but annotated POJOs. You can easily test an EJB bean—even with its injection points.

```
@Singleton

@Path("hitsperday")

public class DailyStatisticsCalculator {

    @EJB

    Hits hits;
```

110

```
@PersistenceContext

EntityManager em;

//...
}
```

Listing 62: An EJB Bean with Injection Points

The injection points from Listing 62 can be mocked out with standard Java SE tools. You need a single `Mockito.mock` (http://www.mockito.org) invocation for each dependency (see Listing 63).

```
class DailyStatisticsCalculatorTest extends JUnitSuite with
MockitoSugar with ShouldMatchersForJUnit{

  var cut: DailyStatisticsCalculator = _

  @Before

  def setUp: Unit = {

    cut = new DailyStatisticsCalculator()

    cut.hits = mock[Hits]

    cut.em = mock[EntityManager]

  }
```

Listing 63: Mocked-Out Dependencies

Only in rare cases is your business logic mainly based on container services. The `Configuration` mechanism as well as `LoggerProducer` rely on CDI producers and dependency injection. A unit test with a mocked-out environment for the `com.abien.xray.business.configuration.boundary.Configuration` class could validate only whether a configuration entry is found in the internal data structure (`HashMap`). You would test only the `java.util.HashMap` implementation, not your code.

Far more interesting is the verification of the injection and Convention over Configuration mechanism. To test the container services, you need a container. You could, of course, deploy your application to the integration server and test the functionality in a real world environment. However, a far better approach is a test inside the container with only a limited set of classes in an isolated environment. With an embeddable container, dedicated test classes can be introduced to validate a particular aspect of the system. Such a test class would not be deployed with production code and would be used only in the test phase.

`com.abien.xray.business.configuration.boundary.Configurable` was exclusively developed for performing integration tests. The class `Configurable` consists of injected fields. Their content will be validated during the integration tests to verify the injection mechanism (see Listing 64).

```java
@Singleton
public class Configurable {
    @Inject
    private String version;
    @Inject
    private String notExistingAndEmpty;
    @Inject
    private boolean debug;
    @Inject
    private int answer;

    public String getVersion() {
        return version;
    }

    public String getNotExistingAndEmpty() {
        return notExistingAndEmpty;
    }

    public int getAnswer() {
        return answer;
    }

    public boolean isDebug() {
        return debug;
    }
}
```

Listing 64: An Injection Dummy

The class Configurable resides in the src/test/java package and is not deployed into production.

Configuration as well as LoggerProducer are based on CDI and used by EJB beans. In contrast to the EJB specification, there is no standardized way to boot the CDI container outside the server. The problem is solved by an open source project, Arquillian (http://www.jboss.org/arquillian), which not only boots the container, but also allows the injection of managed beans and EJB beans into unit test classes (see Listing 65).

```java
import
com.abien.xray.business.configuration.control.ConfigurationProvider;

import org.jboss.arquillian.api.Deployment;

import org.jboss.arquillian.junit.Arquillian;

import org.jboss.shrinkwrap.api.ArchivePaths;

import org.jboss.shrinkwrap.api.ShrinkWrap;

import org.jboss.shrinkwrap.api.asset.ByteArrayAsset;

import org.jboss.shrinkwrap.api.spec.JavaArchive;

import org.junit.Test;

import org.junit.runner.RunWith;

import javax.inject.Inject;

import java.util.Set;

import static org.hamcrest.core.Is.*;

import static org.junit.Assert.*;


@RunWith(Arquillian.class)
public class ConfigurationIT {

    @Inject
    Configurable configurable;


    @Inject
    Configuration configuration;


    @Deployment
    public static JavaArchive createArchive() {
        return ShrinkWrap.create(JavaArchive.class, "xray.jar").
                addClasses(Configuration.class).
```

```
                addClasses(Configurable.class).
                addClasses(ConfigurationProvider.class).
                addManifestResource(
                        new ByteArrayAsset("<beans/>".getBytes()),
                        ArchivePaths.create("beans.xml"));
    }


    @Test
    public void configurableInjection() {
        assertNotNull(this.configurable);
    }



    @Test
    public void customConfigurationNotExist(){
            assertFalse(this.configuration.doesCustomConfigurationExist
());
    }


    @Test
    public void versionInjection() {
        assertNotNull(this.configurable.getVersion());
    }
    @Test
    public void notExistingParameter() {
        assertNull(this.configurable.getNotExistingAndEmpty());
        Set<String> unconfiguredFields =
this.configuration.getUnconfiguredFields();
        assertNotNull(unconfiguredFields);
        assertThat(unconfiguredFields.size(), is(2));
    }
    @Test
    public void booleanInjection(){
```

```
        assertFalse(this.configurable.isDebug());

    }

}
```

Listing 65: Container Bootstrapping in Unit Test

Arquillian not only performs the test, but it also builds the archive in a method annotated with `@Deployment`. You can pick and choose classes that should belong to the on-the-fly created WAR file or JAR file and, thus, the test setup. This is especially convenient for testing optional, ambiguous, or unsatisfied dependencies. The `ConfigurationProvider` class relies heavily on optional dependencies and was also tested with Arquillian.

The test class `ConfigurationIT` ("IT" stands for "IntegrationTest") deploys in the method `createArchive`, the `Configuration`, `Configurable`, and a `ConfigurationProvider`. Java EE components and, therefore, the singleton EJB beans `Configurable` and `Configuration` are injected directly into the `ConfigurationIT` class. `ConfigurationIT` behaves in the unit test as if it were deployed to an application server as an EJB beans or CDI managed bean.

The injection of dependent instances is performed before the execution of the test methods, so you can just work with the references because they would be initialized locally in `@Before` methods.

To activate the dependency injection for your unit tests you need to declare Arquillian as the test runner: `@RunWith(Arquillian.class)`.

Arquillian is maintained in the Maven Repository. To use it with GlassFish, you need to declare a few Maven dependencies (see Listing 66).

```
        <dependency>

            <groupId>org.glassfish.extras</groupId>

            <artifactId>glassfish-embedded-all</artifactId>

            <version>3.0.1</version>

            <scope>provided</scope>

        </dependency>

        <dependency>

            <groupId>org.jboss.arquillian</groupId>

            <artifactId>arquillian-junit</artifactId>

            <version>1.0.0.Alpha4</version>

            <scope>test</scope>
```

```
    </dependency>
    <!-- glassfish container -->
    <dependency>
        <groupId>org.jboss.arquillian.container</groupId>
        <artifactId>arquillian-glassfish-embedded-3</artifactId>
        <version>1.0.0.Alpha4</version>
        <scope>test</scope>
    </dependency>
```

Listing 66: Maven Declaration for Arquillian

Arquillian comes with an adapter layer that abstracts from a concrete application server implementation. You could run the same test code against several application servers just by exchanging a single dependency in `pom.xml`. This can be achieved easily with Maven profiles.

I tested the injection of `XRayLogger` similarly. A class `LogUser` was introduced just as an injection helper for test purposes (see Listing 67) but it was not deployed with the application.

```
public class LogUser {
    @Inject
    private XRayLogger LOG;
    public boolean isLogInjected(){
        return (LOG != null);
    }
    public XRayLogger getLogger() {
        return LOG;
    }
}
```

Listing 67: Helper Class for Dependency Injection Testing

The `LogUser` class declares an `XRayLogger` field and annotates it with `@Inject`. The injection of the expected `XRayLogger` type is verified in the `LoggerProducerIT` test (see Listing 68).

```
@RunWith(Arquillian.class)
public class LoggerProducerIT {
    @Inject
    LogUser logUser;
```

```java
    @Inject

    Configuration configuration;

    @Deployment

    public static JavaArchive createTestArchive() {

            return ShrinkWrap.create(JavaArchive.class,
"loggerproducer.jar").
                    addClasses(LogUser.class, LoggerProducer.class,
Configuration.class, ConfigurationProvider.class,
DebugConfigurationProvider.class, DevNullLogger.class,
DelegatingLogger.class).
                    addManifestResource(
                            new ByteArrayAsset("<beans/>".getBytes()),
                            ArchivePaths.create("beans.xml"));

    }


    @Test

    public void logInjected() {

        assertTrue(logUser.isLogInjected());

    }


    @Test

    public void loggerNameCorrespondsToClassNameNoDebug() {

        XRayLogger xRayLogger = logUser.getLogger();

        assertTrue(xRayLogger instanceof DelegatingLogger);

        Logger logger = xRayLogger.getLogger();

        String actual = logger.getName();

        String expected = LogUser.class.getName();

        assertThat(actual, is(expected));


    }

}
```

Listing 68: XRayLogger Injection in an Integration Test

Both `Configuration` and `LogUser` are injected into the `LoggerProducerIT` class. In the method `loggerNameCorrespondsToClassNameNoDebug`, the configuration-dependent injection of the `XRayLogger` realization is validated. It is an easy task because `LoggerProducerIT` has direct access to `LogUser` as well as `Configuration`. In the method `createTestArchive`, `DebugConfigurationProvider` is deployed, which sets the value of the `debug` entry to `true` (see Listing 69).

```
public class DebugConfigurationProvider implements
ConfigurationProvider{


    @Override

    public Map<String, String> getConfiguration() {

        return new HashMap<String, String>(){{

            put("debug", "true");

        }};

    }

}
```

Listing 69: Debug Configuration Helper

Also, `DebugConfigurationProvider` was developed exclusively for test purposes. The source code resides in `src/test/java` and was deployed only into the test environment, not production. With Arquillian, you can selectively deploy classes in the setup phase of a unit test, which makes the testing of advanced dependency injection possible. The behavior of unsatisfied or ambiguous dependencies is easily testable. There is one caveat with this approach. The creation of the archive, as well as the deployment, happens once for each test class. For tests with different setups (such as testing different `ConfigurationProviders`), you have to create a unit test class for each deployment unit with a different set of classes.

Accidental Performance Improvement of Factor 250

Watching the monitoring output of `com.abien.xray.business.monitoring.PerformanceAuditor`, I noticed the poor performance of the following methods: `Hits.persistReferersCache` and `Hits.persistHitsCache`. Their execution took around 50 seconds in contrast to the remaining methods' performance, which was below 20 ms.

However, both critical methods were executed every five minutes sequentially. Furthermore, the x-ray design ensured that there were no other parallel writers active at the same time. Asynchronous execution of these methods initiated by a timer makes such slow execution absolutely acceptable. X-ray is storing its state in the Hypersonic (hsqldb) database (http://hsqldb.org) in unoptimized "Text" tables (http://www.hsqldb.org/doc/guide/ch06.html).

X-ray had to update a few thousand hits and about 50 thousand referers every five minutes. In this context, the performance is not that bad. Nevertheless, long transactions whose length is dependent on the total number of records might cause trouble in the long run. Transactions that are too long lead to timeouts and, thus, rollbacks, which could lead to data loss. At the same time, it would be interesting to know how many records are cached and become dirty between the flushes.

I met both requirements by adding an additional layer of indirection and introducing the class HitsCache. I factored out the cache previously maintained in the Hits singleton EJB bean into a dedicated HitsCache (see Listing 70).

```
public class HitsCache {
    private ConcurrentHashMap<String, AtomicLong> hits = null;
    private ConcurrentSkipListSet<String> dirtyKeys;

    public HitsCache(Map<String, AtomicLong> hits) {
        this.hits = new ConcurrentHashMap<String, AtomicLong>(hits);
        this.dirtyKeys = new ConcurrentSkipListSet<String>();
    }

    public HitsCache() {
        this(new HashMap<String, AtomicLong>());
    }

    public long increase(String uniqueAction){
        this.dirtyKeys.add(uniqueAction);
        hits.putIfAbsent(uniqueAction, new AtomicLong());
        AtomicLong hitCount = hits.get(uniqueAction);
        return hitCount.incrementAndGet();
    }
```

```java
    public ConcurrentHashMap<String, AtomicLong> getCache() {
        return hits;
    }


    public Map<String, AtomicLong> getChangedEntriesAndClear() {
        Map<String,AtomicLong> changedValues = new HashMap<String,
AtomicLong>();
        for (String dirtyKey : dirtyKeys) {
            dirtyKeys.remove(dirtyKey);
            changedValues.put(dirtyKey, hits.get(dirtyKey));
        }
        return changedValues;
    }

    public int getCacheSize(){
        return this.hits.size();
    }

    public int getDirtyEntriesCount(){
        return this.dirtyKeys.size();
    }

    public void clear() {
        hits.clear();
        dirtyKeys.clear();
    }
}
```

Listing 70: Encapsulation of the Cache and Dirty Detection

Also, with the encapsulation of the hits and referers caches into dedicated classes, the complexity of the Hits class was slightly reduced. After the refactoring, Hits delegates to the cache implementation (see Listing 71).

```
public class Hits{

...

  long storeHitStatistics(String uniqueAction) {
        return this.hitStatistics.increase(uniqueAction);

    }
  public void persistHitsCache() {
        hitStore.store(hitStatistics.getChangedEntriesAndClear());

    }

...

}
```

Listing 71: Persisting the Dirty Hits

Instead of updating all entries and relying on the JPA implementation-specific optimizations, only the changed entries computed by the caches are passed to `EntityManager`. This improved the performance dramatically. Even during peaks, the slowest execution of the `Hits.persistReferersCache` and `Hits.persistHitsCache` methods took 173 ms, which is about 250 times faster than the unoptimized version.

According to the following Donald Knuth quote (http://en.wikiquote.org/wiki/Donald_Knuth), this optimization was not driven by the need for premature performance improvement, but for monitoring.

"We should forget about small efficiencies, say about 97% of the time: premature optimization is the root of all evil. Yet we should not pass up our opportunities in that critical 3%."

To be able to monitor the caches, they had to be better encapsulated. With the availability of the "deltas" between the flushes, the optimization turned out to be a one-liner. Here, the performance gain was more of an accident than an intention.

Introducing caches without measuring the performance is dangerous. Caches are accessed concurrently, and they have to store entries for faster access. They have to maintain consistency, and they also need to deal with memory consumption efficiently. In fact, naively implemented custom caches often introduce locking and memory issues.

X-ray Consumer Client

5

X-ray services were built as a quick hack to watch some strange activities on my blog in real time. It turned out that the majority of all statistics might also be interesting for the blog visitors. So, I introduced an additional REST client to access the x-ray services via HTTP/REST and expose the interesting data directly to blog visitors in real time.

REST Client in a Class

The `x-ray-services` module already exposes interesting statistics as REST services. The statistics were initially intended for private use, but it was far more convenient to monitor the statistics through the public blog.adam-bien.com page, rather than using private access for that purpose. Furthermore, the popularity of blog posts and trends might also be interesting to blog visitors.

There is no direct client-side support for REST in Java EE 6, so I either had to use an existing client library or implement a standalone client. The x-ray-client module is shipped with the Roller blogging software. To mitigate other software interfering with the Roller software and to simplify the installation process, I implemented a standalone REST client without any external dependencies. It sounds complex, but the implementation turned out to be surprisingly simple (see Listing 72).

```
public class XRay {

    private String baseUrl;
    public final static String HITS_PER_HOUR = "hitsperhour";
    public final static String MOST_POPULAR = "mostpopular";
    public final static String HITS_PER_MINUTE = "hitsperminute";
```

```java
    public final static String TOTAL_HITS = "hits";

    public final static String HITS_FOR_URI = "hits/";

    public final static String TRENDING = "trending?max=5";

    public final static String TODAY_HITS = "hitsperday/today";


    public final static String YESTERDAY_HITS = "hitsperday/
yesterday";

    private final static Logger LOG = Logger.getLogger
(XRay.class.getName());

    private static final int TIMEOUT_IN_MS = 100;


    public XRay(String url) {

        this.baseUrl = url;

    }


    public String getHitsPerHour() {

        String uri = getUrl(HITS_PER_HOUR);

        return getContent(uri);

    }


    public String getTotalHits(){

        String uri = getUrl(TOTAL_HITS);

        return getContent(uri);

    }


//some getters omitted


    public String getHitsForPost(String post) {

        String uri = getUrl(HITS_FOR_URI);

        String encoded;

        try {

            encoded = URLEncoder.encode(post, "UTF-8");

        } catch (UnsupportedEncodingException e) {
```

```
            LOG.log(Level.SEVERE, "Cannot encode URI: {0} Reason:
{1}", new Object[]{post, e});

                return "--";

        }

        String postURL = uri + encoded;

        return getContent(postURL);

    }

    String getUrl(String command) {

        return baseUrl + command;

    }

    String getContent(String uri){

            try {

            URL url = new URL(uri);

            return getContent(url);

        } catch (Exception ex) {

            LOG.log(Level.SEVERE, "Cannot connect to X-Ray-Services:
{0} Reason: {1}", new Object[]{uri, ex});

                return "--";

        }

    }


String getContent(URL url) throws IOException {

        URLConnection urlConnection = url.openConnection();

        urlConnection.setConnectTimeout(TIMEOUT_IN_MS);

        urlConnection.setReadTimeout(TIMEOUT_IN_MS);

        InputStream stream = urlConnection.getInputStream();

        BufferedReader br = new BufferedReader(new InputStreamReader
(stream));

        String line;

        StringBuilder content = new StringBuilder("");

        while ((line = br.readLine()) != null) {

            content.append(line);

        }
```

```
        br.close();

        return content.toString();

    }

}
```

Listing 72: A "GET" REST Client in a Class

The entire HTTP functionality was encapsulated in the method getContent. The getContent method opens an HTTP connection, puts the content of a passed URL into a string and eventually returns it. The remaining methods just wrap the getContent(URL) method and republish the method under a more convenient name.

An external REST library would eliminate the getContent method but would also introduce external dependencies to REST frameworks. Because the statistics are exclusively invoked with the GET method, the implementation of an HTTP/REST client is trivial. In a more sophisticated use case, the use of an external library would be far more appropriate.

Timeouts Are Crucial

As already mentioned, x-ray-services must not have any impact on the stability of the blogging software. Statistics are an optional feature; an x-ray crash should not affect the availability of the blog. This reasoning leads to another conclusion: x-ray services should be optional.

```
    String getContent(String uri){

            try {

            URL url = new URL(uri);

            return getContent(url);

        } catch (Exception ex) {

            LOG.log(Level.SEVERE, "Cannot connect to x-ray services:
{0} Reason: {1}", new Object[]{uri, ex});

            return "--";

        }

    }
```

Listing 73: Exception Swallowing for Availability

Meeting this requirement is surprisingly simple. All exceptions have to be caught and ignored. A "—" character is returned if something went wrong during the HTTP communication. For the blog visitor, a "double hyphen" looks like a natural sign indicating the unavailability of the statistics. In general, visitors are more interested in the blog content, than in statistics. So it is OK to make the statistics optional.

Just catching an exception does not ensure the stability of the system. Deadlocks and "livelocks" (http://en.wikipedia.org/wiki/Deadlock#Livelock) can still occur, which would lead to infinite blocking calls. If x-ray becomes overloaded and responds slowly, that would affect the performance and scalability of the x-ray client (blogging software) as well. The read timeout in `java.net.URLConnection` allows the configuration of the maximum-wait time:

```
String getContent(URL url) throws IOException {

        URLConnection urlConnection = url.openConnection();

        urlConnection.setConnectTimeout(TIMEOUT_IN_MS);

        urlConnection.setReadTimeout(TIMEOUT_IN_MS);

//...

}
```

After the specified period, a `java.net.SocketTimeoutException` is raised, which again leads to the acceptable "—" result. Aggressive timeout settings improve the situation significantly. In fact, it is possible to redeploy the x-ray backend in production without affecting the page rendering or degrading the performance.

X-ray was deployed with a timeout setting of 100 ms. During normal operations, the timeout was never reached. In the worst-case scenario, visitors had to wait 100 ms for x-ray to return a "—" character, which is absolutely acceptable.

In enterprise projects, timeouts are the easiest solution for the resolution of deadlocks. You should define sensible timeouts for each resource and ask yourself what should happen in the event of a timeout. In most cases, the question cannot be answered by a developer; rather, it must be answered by the product owner or business analysts.

Velocity Integration

Roller uses the Apache project Velocity (http://velocity.apache.org/) for site rendering. Velocity is a templating engine written in Java. It comes with its own language and can directly access the value of Java properties. You can directly traverse the properties by using the property names omitting the "get" prefix.

```
Yesterday's hits: $xraymodel.xray.yesterdayHits<br/>

Today's hits: $xraymodel.xray.todayHits<br/>

Post reads / hour: $xraymodel.xray.hitsPerHour<br/>
```

```
Top posts:<br/>

$xraymodel.xray.mostPopularAsHtml
```

Listing 74: X-ray Services Velocity Integration

In Listing 74, an instance with the name `xraymodel` is traversed. Its method `getXray()` is invoked, which returns an object (the `XRay` from Listing 72) with the `getYesterdayHits`, `getTodayHits` and `getHitsPerHour` methods. `XRay` results can be directly merged with the Roller page.

You could similarly integrate a REST client with a JSF page. You would have to expose `XRay` with a CDI managed bean denoted with `@Named("xraymodel")`, and you could integrate the interesting property directly into a JSF page using an EL expression: #{xraymodel.xray.yesterdayHits}.

Roller Integration

The x-ray/Roller integration is achieved with the classic Gang of Four Adapter pattern (http://en.wikipedia.org/wiki/Adapter_pattern). An adapter implements a compatible interface and delegates all calls to the incompatible interface (see Listing 75).

```
import org.apache.roller.weblogger.ui.rendering.model.Model;

public class XRayModel implements Model{

    public static final String XRAYMODEL_NAME = "xraymodel";


    private Map configuration;

    private XRay xray;

    public final static String URL = "http://192.168.0.50:5380/x-ray/
resources/";

    public final static String XRAYURL = "XRAY-URL";


    @Override
    public void init(Map map) {

        this.configuration = map;

        this.xray = initializeXRay(this.configuration);

    }


    @Override
```

```java
public String getModelName() {
    return XRAYMODEL_NAME;
}


public XRay getXray(){
    return xray;
}


String extractUrl(Map map){
    if(map == null){
        return URL;
    }
    String url = (String) map.get(XRAYURL);
    if(url != null){
        return url;
    }
    return URL;
}


XRay initializeXRay(Map map) {
    String url = extractUrl(map);
    return new XRay(url);
}

}
```

Listing 75: X-ray Integration with Adapter

In contrast to a pure Adapter pattern implementation, the XRayModel class does not delegate anything to the XRay API class; rather, it exposes the XRay class with a getter. The overridden method getModelName returns the name to be used in the template to access the model. The first segment in the path $xraymodel.xray.mostPopularAsHtml is the return value of the getModelName method, the next is the XRayModel#getXray() method, and the last is the property of the XRay object itself.

The XRayModel class together with the XRay client are packaged in a self-containing JAR file and deployed together with the Roller application.

Development Process

6

Development of enterprise applications shouldn't be any different than development of plain Java SE applications. Java SE applications are built according to the "Write, Compile, Test, Run" cycle, which should also be applicable to Java EE applications. Unfortunately, because of dependencies on external resources and server runtime, running and testing an enterprise application without any improvement takes too long. Also setup, configuration, and deployment are too complex to be performed in an ad-hoc manner manually. By splitting the testing into several manageable chunks, and introducing automated setup, configuration, and deployment, you can get remarkably close to a build cycle of a plain Java SE application.

A fully automated build and deployment cycle is the first step towards the DevOps idea (http://en.wikipedia.org/wiki/DevOps), where the boundary between developers and operations blurs.

The separation between developers and operations is rather artificial. A developer has to set up the environment for development and test and could reuse his automated process for building the integration environment and even the production environment as well. DevOps tries to automate every reasonable step and treat the recipe as code. A fully automated process is repeatable, so you can apply the same parameterized automation for local, test, integration and even production environments.

Build and Deployment

X-ray was developed with NetBeans 7 (Java EE edition, http://www.netbeans.org), tested with GlassFish v3.1, and built with Maven 3 as a Java EE 6 project. It consists of eight Maven projects (some are prototypes). The back-end code discussed in this book comes from the `x-ray-services` module. The `x-ray-services` module is a self-contained Java EE 6 WAR file with REST, EJB beans, CDI managed beans, and JPA 2 entities.

I created the structure of the Java EE 6 project with a Maven plug-in called "archetype" (http://maven.apache.org/archetype/maven-archetype-plugin/). Archetype is a wizard-like plug-in that creates preconfigured projects for various technologies. For the initial creation of a Java EE 6 WAR file, projects in the webapp-javaee6 artifact can be used (see Listing 76).

```
mvn -Darchetype.interactive=true -
DarchetypeGroupId=org.codehaus.mojo.archetypes -
DarchetypeArtifactId=webapp-javaee6 archetype:generate
```

Listing 76: Java EE 6 Project Generation with Maven

There is even a more convenient way to create a project by just skipping all parameters and executing the plain `mvn archetype:generate` command. This starts an interactive wizard, lists all available archetypes, and prompts you for a number:

...

```
256: remote -> webapp-j2ee14 (J2EE 1.4 web application archetype)
```

257: remote -> webapp-javaee6 (Archetype for a web application using Java EE 6.)

```
258: remote -> webapp-jee5 (JEE 5 web application archetype)
```

...

Choosing "257" initiates the generation of an empty Java EE 6 WAR project, which can be opened with any Maven-capable IDE. You shouldn't use the chosen number for automatic generation of projects in the background, because the number can change at any time. In fact, it already changed to "260" during the writing of this book.

I created the x-ray services project with the NetBeans 7 wizard, which uses the same archetypes (see Listing 76) to create the `x-ray-services` project initially. By using the NetBeans 7 wizard, your project is truly independent of any IDE; you can switch back and forth between IDEs as you like. Listing 77 shows a slightly extended `pom.xml` with test dependencies created by the `archetype:generate` plug-in:

```
<project xmlns="http://maven.apache.org/POM/4.0.0" xmlns:xsi="http://
www.w3.org/2001/XMLSchema-instance"

        xsi:schemaLocation="http://maven.apache.org/POM/4.0.0 http://
maven.apache.org/maven-v4_0_0.xsd">

    <modelVersion>4.0.0</modelVersion>

    <groupId>com.abien.xray</groupId>

    <artifactId>x-ray-services</artifactId>

    <packaging>war</packaging>

    <version>1.0-SNAPSHOT</version>

    <name>x-ray-services Java EE 6 Webapp</name>
```

```xml
<url>http://maven.apache.org</url>
<repositories>
    <repository>
        <id>java.net</id>
        <name>Repository hosting the Glassfish</name>
        <url>http://download.java.net/maven/glassfish/</url>
    </repository>
</repositories>
<pluginRepositories>
    <pluginRepository>
        <id>maven2.java.net</id>
        <name>Java.net Repository for Maven 2</name>
        <url>http://download.java.net/maven/2</url>
    </pluginRepository>
</pluginRepositories>
<dependencies>
    <dependency>
        <groupId>org.glassfish.extras</groupId>
        <artifactId>glassfish-embedded-all</artifactId>
        <version>3.0.1</version>
        <scope>provided</scope>
    </dependency>
</dependencies>
<!-- test dependencies omitted -->
<build>
    <plugins>
        <plugin>
            <groupId>org.apache.maven.plugins</groupId>
            <artifactId>maven-compiler-plugin</artifactId>
            <version>2.3.2</version>
            <configuration>
                <source>1.6</source>
```

```
            <target>1.6</target>
        </configuration>
    </plugin>
    <plugin>
        <groupId>org.apache.maven.plugins</groupId>
        <artifactId>maven-war-plugin</artifactId>
        <version>2.1</version>
        <configuration>
            <failOnMissingWebXml>false</failOnMissingWebXml>
        </configuration>
    </plugin>
    <plugin>
        <groupId>org.apache.maven.plugins</groupId>
        <artifactId>maven-failsafe-plugin</artifactId>
        <version>2.7.1</version>
    </plugin>
  </plugins>
  <finalName>x-ray</finalName>
</build>
</project>
```

Listing 77: Complete Java EE 6 WAR Build Configuration pom.xml

By default, x-ray-services is built with the standard mvn (clean) install command. The result is an x-ray.war file that can be deployed by dropping it into the glassfish/domains/x-ray/autodeploy folder. A file system copy works, but doesn't give you any feedback about the deployment's success.

```
#!/bin/bash
GLASSFISH_HOME=[PATH TO GLASSFISH]/glassfish3.1-current
XRAY_WAR=[PATH TO PROJECT]/x-ray/x-ray-services/target/x-ray.war
$GLASSFISH_HOME/bin/asadmin --port 5348 deploy --force $XRAY_WAR
```

Listing 78: WAR Deployment with Command Line Interface

Instead of using a simple copy, GlassFish's asadmin command line interface is a far better alternative for application deployment. The asadmin command blocks until the application is deployed and it informs you about the outcome. An executable bash script wraps the `asadmin` command and makes it reusable (see Listing 78).

NetBeans also supports GlassFish deployments with Maven directly from the IDE, so the deployment script described here is used only for automated deployments to an integration environment or during load tests. No IDE-specific extensions are required. NetBeans 7 uses the plain `pom.xml` without any specific files or extensions.

Continuous Integration and QA

To perform the build in a clearly defined environment, Hudson (http://java.net/projects/hudson) and Jenkins (http://jenkins-ci.org) use exactly the same project file as the IDE (`pom.xml`) and execute the build on the central server.

A Mercurial (http://mercurial.selenic.com/) or Git (http://git-scm.com/) "push" (or an SVN commit) sends a GET request to the Hudson or Jenkins API, which initiates a fresh checkout. The `changegroup` hook in the Mercurial configuration `.hg/hgrc` updates the "master" repository to the current release and starts the Hudson or Jenkins build job using an HTTP interface (see Listing 79). The `changegroup` hook is activated on every push from a local developer repository to the master repository. The master repository is usually configured as the "default push target" in each developer repository.

```
[hooks]
changegroup = hg update >&2
changegroup.hudson = curl http:/[HUDSON_HOST]/hudson/job/x-ray/build?
delay=0sec
```

Listing 79: Hook Setup for Mercurial from .hg/hgrc

Hudson manages the dependencies between jobs. A successful job triggers the action specified in the Post-build Actions section of the Hudson UI (see Figure 3), for example, the execution of the next job.

Build

Maven Version	maven3.0 ▲▼
Root POM	x-ray-assembly/pom.xml ⑦
Goals and options	clean install ⑦

[Advanced...]

Build Settings

☐ E-mail Notification   ⑦

Post-build Actions

☐ Aggregate downstream test results   ⑦

☐ Archive the artifacts   ⑦

☑ Build other projects   ⑦

Projects to build   x-ray-integration

              ☐ Trigger even if the build is unstable

☐ Publish Fitnesse results report

☐ Deploy artifacts to Maven repository   ⑦

[Save]

Figure 3: Initial X-ray Build in Hudson

All jobs are executed in the following sequence (see Figure 4):

- x-ray (initial build and unit test execution triggered by a post-commit hook, for example, the changegroup hook in Mercurial)

- x-ray-integration (execution of local integration tests with embedded container and JPA persistence)

- x-ray-setup-server (GlassFish installation, setup, and restart)

- x-ray-deploy (deployment to integration environment)

- x-ray-setup-fitnesse (build and deployment of fixture code; optional)

- x-ray-fitnesse (execution of functional tests)

- x-ray-sonar (static code analysis)

Hudson initially checks out all the sources, builds the project, and performs unit tests (see Figure 3). All unit tests access a mocked-out environment, which significantly speeds up the build. A whole build with unit tests takes less than 5 seconds. Successful completion of the x-ray job automatically triggers the execution of the next stage: the x-ray-integration job. x-ray-integration acts on the same sources but executes mvn failsafe:integration-test.

136

S	W	Job ↓	Last Success	Last Failure	Last Duration	
●	☀	x-ray	1 hr 27 min (#80)	2 hr 47 min (#75)	1 min 2 sec	◉
●	⛅	x-ray-deploy	1 hr 20 min (#20)	1 hr 22 min (#19)	19 sec	◉
●	☀	x-ray-fitnesse	8 days 17 hr (#7)	8 days 17 hr (#1)	0.52 sec	◉
●	☀	x-ray-integration	1 hr 26 min (#22)	3 mo 1 day (#1)	2 min 31 sec	◉
●	☁	x-ray-setup-server	1 hr 23 min (#17)	1 hr 27 min (#16)	20 sec	◉
●	⛅	x-ray-sonar	8 days 5 hr (#32)	8 days 5 hr (#30)	3 min 15 sec	◉

Figure 4: X-ray Jobs in Hudson

All test classes ending with "IT" (for Integration Test) are executed in the x-ray-integration phase. Although the JUnit and ScalaTest (http://www.scalatest.org/) frameworks are still used, the test classes do not mock out the test environment any more. The persistence, or even the whole application server (with Arquillian), is started in process.

After the successful execution of all integration tests, a fresh instance of the application server is created with a simple bash script (see 80) wrapped as Hudson job x-ray-setup-server.

```
#!/bin/bash

GLASSFISH_HOME=[PATH_TO_GLASSFISH]/glassfish3.1-current

$GLASSFISH_HOME/bin/asadmin delete-domain x-ray

$GLASSFISH_HOME/bin/asadmin create-domain --portbase 5300 --
nopassword=true x-ray

cp ./jdbc-drivers/hsql2/* $GLASSFISH_HOME/glassfish/domains/x-ray/lib/
ext


$GLASSFISH_HOME/bin/asadmin start-domain x-ray

$GLASSFISH_HOME/bin/asadmin create-jdbc-connection-pool  --port 5348
--datasourceclassname org.hsqldb.jdbc.JDBCDataSource --restype
javax.sql.ConnectionPoolDataSource --property
"User=****:Password=****:Database=jdbc\\:hsqldb\\:hsql\\://localhost\
\:9093/x-ray" hsqldb

$GLASSFISH_HOME/bin/asadmin create-jdbc-resource --port 5348 --
connectionpoolid hsqldb jdbc/hitscounter
```

Listing 80: Automatic Domain Creation

`x-ray-services` is deployed (with the already discussed `asadmin` deploy command wrapped as the `x-ray-deploy` Hudson job) into the freshly created and started GlassFish `x-ray` domain. After the deployment of the application, the `x-ray-fitnesse` job executes the functional tests remotely.

Fitnesse + Java EE = Good Friends

Functional tests are similar to integration tests (and sometimes even unit tests), but they are dedicated to stakeholders with domain or business responsibilities. Integration tests are driven by developers and functional tests are driven by product owners or business experts.

The primary goal of functional tests is the verification of the correct functionality of the system. Fitnesse (http://fitnesse.org) is an excellent tool for bridging the gap between developers and domain experts. Domain experts are able to maintain the specification and execute the tests without any developer intervention.

Fitnesse is a "wiki on steroids" that comes with its own ready-to-use Web server. A wiki page can be created, versioned, and maintained directly from the UI. Wiki tables are treated as "bidirectional" test data (fixture). The input is parsed and passed to a declared fixture class. Verification is performed and the actual outcome is compared with the expected result. Successful tests are highlighted as green cells, failed tests are red, and exceptions are yellow (see Figure 5).

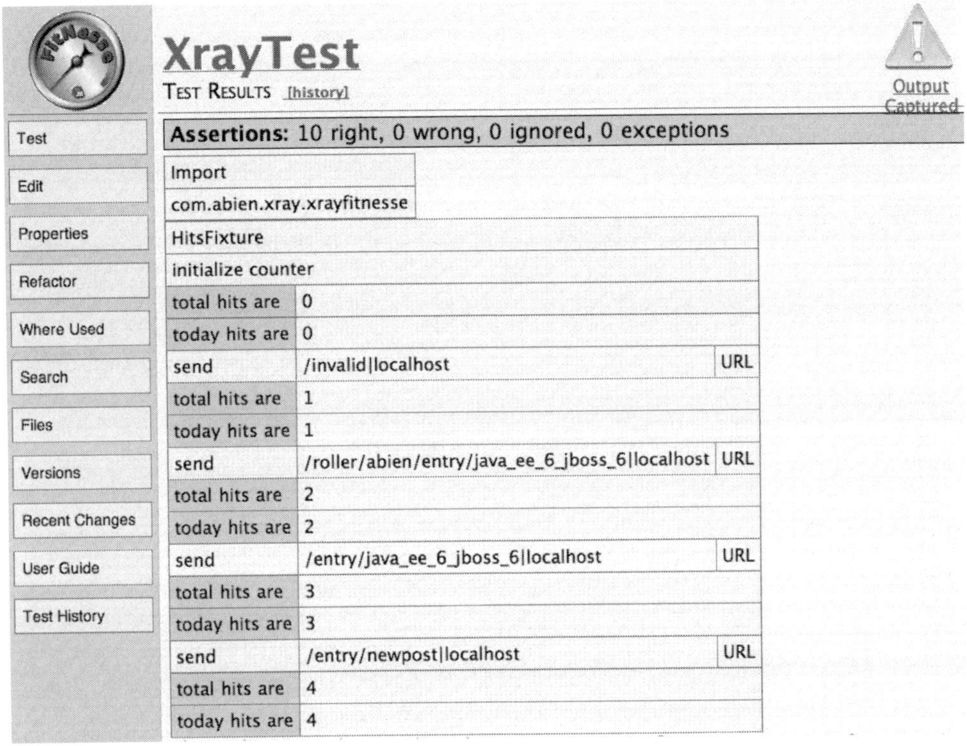

Figure 5: Fitnesse Wiki Table

Usually, you would start with the creation of a page just by adding the name of the page directly in the URL, for example, http://localhost:8080/MyNewTest. Fitnesse opens an editor, and you can start inputting the test data and verification. Before you start the table creation, you should choose a suitable fixture for your test case. I'm using a DoFixture (http://fitnesse.org/FitNesse.UserGuide.FixtureGallery.FitLibraryFixtures.DoFixture) to invoke the external x-ray-services API. A DoFixture enables a story-like test specification by relying on the Convention over Configuration principle.

The DoFixture class (the glue between the wiki page and your code) must be declared in the table first. You can consider the rows in a wiki table (see Listing 81) as method executions. All methods with the boolean return type are used to compare the results; other methods are just executed.

```
|Import|
```

139

```
|com.abien.xray.xrayfitnesse|

!|HitsFixture|

|initialize counter|

|total hits are  |0|

|today hits are  |0|

|send|/invalid!-|-!localhost|URL|

|total hits are|1|

|today hits are|1|

|send|/roller/abien/entry/java_ee_6_jboss_6!-|-!localhost|URL|

|total hits are|2|

|today hits are|2|

|send|/entry/java_ee_6_jboss_6!-|-!localhost|URL|

|total hits are|3|

|today hits are|3|

|send|/entry/newpost!-|-!localhost|URL|

|total hits are|4|

|today hits are|4|

!path [PATH_TO_FIXTURE]/x-ray-fitnesse-1.0-SNAPSHOT-jar-with-
dependencies.jar
```

Listing 81: Defintion of DoFixture Test

In the first three lines of the wiki table (Listing 81), HitsFixture is declared, and the last line points to the actual JAR file with the implementation. The !path directive is effectively a CLASSPATH extension of the Web server. The path has to include the fixture class with all required dependencies.

The |initialize counter| row performs a single fixture initialization. The remaining rows are used for the actual test. The row |send|/invalid!-|-!localhost|URL| sends an HTTP request to x-ray and the following two rows are used to verify the result:

```
|total hits are|1|

|today hits are|1|
```

The class `HitsFixture` in Listing 82 extends `fitlibrary.DoFixture`. All public methods are directly invoked by the Fitnesse runtime. There is, however, an intended mismatch between the actual method names and the wiki declaration. For example, an action appears in the wiki as "today hits are" and the actual name of the corresponding method is `totalHitsAre (String hits)`. The camel-case (http://en.wikipedia.org/wiki/Camel_case) naming pattern can be transformed to words separated by spaces. The transformed words can even be spread across the cells. The odd cells contain the parts of the name and the even cells contain the parameters.

```
import fitlibrary.DoFixture;

//...

public class HitsFixture extends DoFixture{

    public static final String INTEGRATION_SERVER_URI = "http://
localhost:5380/x-ray/resources/";


    private RESTClient client;

    private XRay ray;


    private long initialTotalHits;

    private long initialTodayHits;



    public HitsFixture() throws MalformedURLException {

        URL url = new URL(INTEGRATION_SERVER_URI+"hits");

        this.client = new RESTClient(url);

        this.ray = new XRay(INTEGRATION_SERVER_URI);

    }


    public void initializeCounter(){

        this.initialTotalHits = Long.parseLong
(this.ray.getTotalHits());
```

```java
        this.initialTodayHits = Long.parseLong
(this.ray.getTodayHits());

    }



    public boolean totalHitsAre(String hits){

        final String totalHits = computeTotalHits
(this.ray.getTotalHits());

        return hits.equals(totalHits);

    }



    public boolean todayHitsAre(String hits){

        final String todayHits = computeTodayHits
(this.ray.getTodayHits());

        return hits.equals(todayHits);

    }



    public void sendURL(String url){

        this.client.put(url, mockHeaders());

    }


Map<String,String> mockHeaders(){

    Map<String,String> map = new HashMap<String,String>();

    map.put("referer", "hugo");

    map.put("user-agent","netscape");

    return map;

}
```

```
    private String computeTotalHits(String hits) {

        return String.valueOf((Long.parseLong(hits) -
this.initialTotalHits));

    }

    private String computeTodayHits(String hits) {

        return String.valueOf((Long.parseLong(hits) -
this.initialTodayHits));

    }

}
```

Listing 82: A DoFixture Implementation

The odd-even cell naming was used for the `public void sendURL(String url)` method. The method appears as `send [method parameter] URL` in the wiki and is fluently readable.

The class `HitsFixture` uses the x-ray probe and the public REST API, or the x-ray client and x-ray Maven dependencies, to communicate with `x-ray-services`. Verifications, as well as HTTP invocations, are executed on the integration server. You could, however, also use Fitnesse to test domain classes in an isolated, mocked-out environment.

I integrated Fitnesse in Hudson as a free-style software project and Fitnesse plug-in (http://wiki.hudson-ci.org/display/HUDSON/Fitnesse+Plugin) (see Figure 6). Hudson communicates with an external Fitnesse server, executes the tests, and aggregates the results.

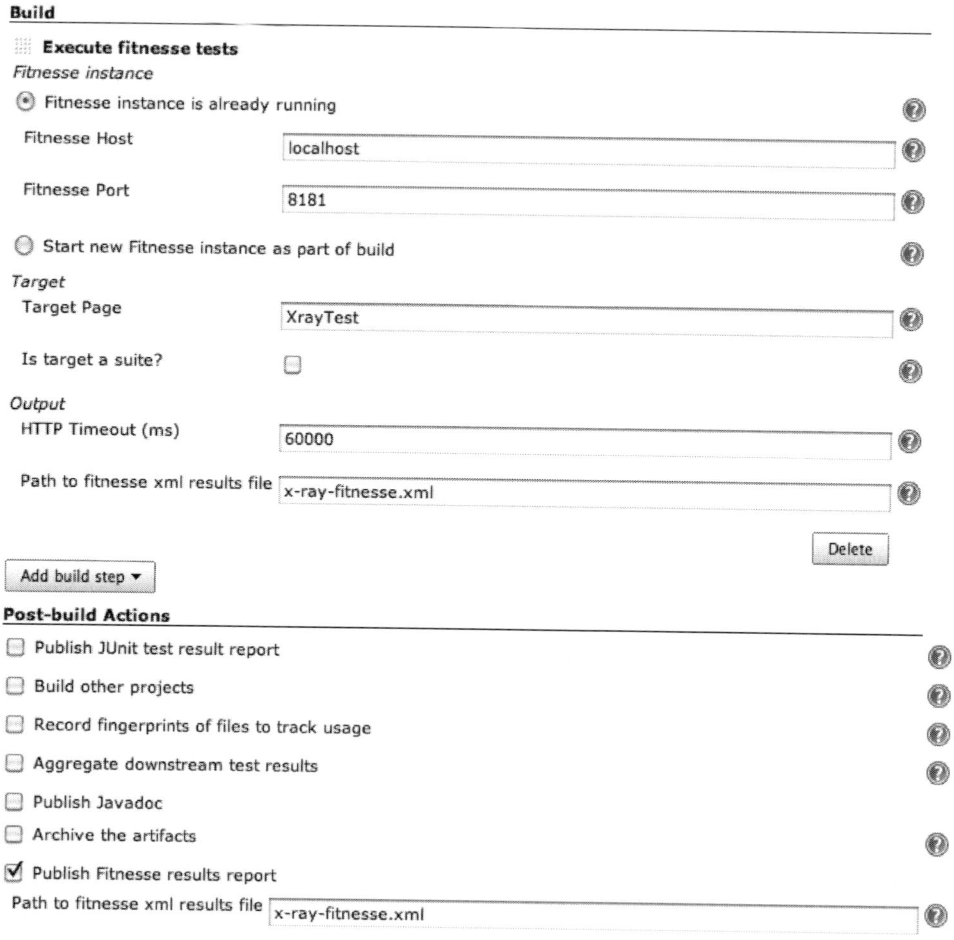

Build

::: **Execute fitnesse tests**

Fitnesse instance

◉ Fitnesse instance is already running   ⑦

    Fitnesse Host   `localhost`   ⑦

    Fitnesse Port   `8181`   ⑦

○ Start new Fitnesse instance as part of build   ⑦

Target

    Target Page   `XrayTest`   ⑦

    Is target a suite?   ☐   ⑦

Output

    HTTP Timeout (ms)   `60000`   ⑦

    Path to fitnesse xml results file   `x-ray-fitnesse.xml`   ⑦

         [Delete]

[Add build step ▼]

Post-build Actions

☐ Publish JUnit test result report   ⑦

☐ Build other projects   ⑦

☐ Record fingerprints of files to track usage   ⑦

☐ Aggregate downstream test results   ⑦

☐ Publish Javadoc

☐ Archive the artifacts   ⑦

☑ Publish Fitnesse results report

    Path to fitnesse xml results file   `x-ray-fitnesse.xml`   ⑦

Figure 6: Fitnesse Configuration in Hudson

Build Your Fitnesse

Fitnesse test code is built and tested as a standalone Maven module. It is packaged as a JAR project (see Listing 83) with the Fitnesse and `fitlibrary` dependencies.

```
<project xmlns="http://maven.apache.org/POM/4.0.0"
xmlns:xsi="http://www.w3.org/2001/XMLSchema-instance"
```

```xml
        xsi:schemaLocation="http://maven.apache.org/POM/4.0.0 http://
maven.apache.org/xsd/maven-4.0.0.xsd">
    <modelVersion>4.0.0</modelVersion>

    <groupId>com.abien.xray</groupId>
    <artifactId>x-ray-fitnesse</artifactId>
    <version>1.0-SNAPSHOT</version>
    <packaging>jar</packaging>

    <name>x-ray-fitnesse</name>
    <url>http://maven.apache.org</url>
    <repositories>
        <repository>
            <id>neuri</id>
            <url>http://maven.neuri.com/</url>
            <releases>
                <enabled>true</enabled>
            </releases>
            <snapshots>
                <enabled>false</enabled>
            </snapshots>
        </repository>
    </repositories>
    <build>
        <plugins>
            <plugin>
                <artifactId>maven-assembly-plugin</artifactId>
                <version>2.2</version>
                <configuration>
                    <descriptorRefs>
                <descriptorRef>jar-with-dependencies</descriptorRef>
                    </descriptorRefs>
```

```xml
                </configuration>
            </plugin>
            <plugin>
                <groupId>org.apache.maven.plugins</groupId>
                <artifactId>maven-compiler-plugin</artifactId>
                <version>2.0.2</version>
                <configuration>
                    <source>1.6</source>
                    <target>1.6</target>
                </configuration>
            </plugin>
        </plugins>
    </build>
    <dependencies>
        <dependency>
            <groupId>org.fitnesse</groupId>
            <artifactId>fitnesse</artifactId>
            <version>20100103</version>
            <scope>provided</scope>
        </dependency>
        <dependency>
            <groupId>org.fitnesse</groupId>
            <artifactId>fitlibrary</artifactId>
            <version>20080812</version>
            <scope>compile</scope>
        </dependency>
        <dependency>
            <groupId>com.abien.xray</groupId>
            <artifactId>x-ray</artifactId>
            <version>1.0-SNAPSHOT</version>
            <scope>compile</scope>
        </dependency>
```

```xml
    <dependency>
        <groupId>com.abien.xray</groupId>
        <artifactId>x-ray-client</artifactId>
        <version>1.0-SNAPSHOT</version>
        <scope>compile</scope>
    </dependency>
    <dependency>
        <groupId>junit</groupId>
        <artifactId>junit</artifactId>
        <version>4.8.2</version>
        <scope>test</scope>
    </dependency>
    </dependencies>
    <properties>
        <project.build.sourceEncoding>UTF-8</
project.build.sourceEncoding>
    </properties>
    </project>
```

Listing 83: Maven Build for Fitnesse

Neither dependency is deployed into the default Maven repository. The Maven repository (http://maven.neuri.com/) contains both libraries and needs to be included in the `<repositories>` section. The Fitnesse Maven build is executed only on demand in case the fixture class (see Listing 82) changes. Implementation of new use cases, or signature changes of the existing methods, would require a build execution and redeployment of the resulting JAR file to the Fitnesse server.

Changes in the internal business logic implementation do not affect the fixture code. `x-ray-fitnesse` could be built easily on a CI server as well. You could insert a new `x-ray-fitnesse-setup` build job before `x-ray-fitnesse` (Figure 4) to build the fixture on every commit. In the case of x-ray, the fixture changes too infrequently to become appropriate for CI, so it is not built on CI for build performance reasons.

Continuous Quality Feedback with Sonar

In the last part of the build code, quality metrics are performed with Sonar (http://www.sonarsource.org), a Maven plug-in that performs several static analysis checks with PMD, FindBugs, Checkstyle, and its own analysis tools. The Sonar plug-in is launched with the `mvn sonar:sonar` command, and the results are presented in a nice looking dashboard.

Sonar (see Figure 2) gives you feedback about the overall code quality. In the real world, absolute numbers are less interesting than overall trends and some indicators, for example, copy and paste detection. An objective indicator of code coverage is the relationship between code coverage and cyclomatic complexity. Sonar even comes with a dedicated "Top Risks" dashboard with appealing visualization (see the "Don't Test Everything" section). It is essential to run Sonar in the main build on every commit. Only then will you get instantaneous feedback about the code quality. The less code quality is measured, the less interesting it becomes to the developer.

After the Sonar execution, the successful build is tagged and could be deployed into production. This step could also be triggered by a "post-commit" hook, but it isn't. X-ray does not run in a cluster, so I could not implement a rolling-update deployment. On a single node, redeployment would be noticeable to the blog visitor, because x-ray wouldn't be available for about 5 seconds. The blog (blog.adam-bien.com) would still be available, but the statistics would not. Furthermore, some statistics, such as daily hits, are not persisted, so they get lost on every redeployment. This is the main reason why new updates are delivered around midnight and they are triggered by Hudson automatically.

Executing all parts of a full build in one step would take too long and would not be accepted by developers. Instant feedback is absolutely necessary for productivity. Unit tests have to be executed in seconds, not minutes. This requires a clean separation between true unit tests and integration tests. The whole build cycle has to be separated into manageable parts, so you get feedback about the execution status of each job.

Git/Mercurial in the Clouds

A distributed version control system (DVCS) (http://en.wikipedia.org/wiki/Distributed_revision_control), such as Mercurial (http://mercurial.selenic.com/) or Git (http://git-scm.com/), initiates the CI process with the push command. The push command synchronizes all recent changes with a remote (sometimes "master") repository.

A CI server listens to the changes and performs a build cycle initiated by a "push." A push is usually performed after several tests and commits to a local repository. This is a substantial difference from SVN, CVS, and other central source code repository tools (http://en.wikipedia.org/wiki/Revision_control). With SVN, every commit initiates a central build; the granularity is substantially finer. Naturally, the quality of push content is usually higher than the quality of a single commit. Also, more "meat" is included in a push compared to a commit.

This makes a DVCS system interesting for pushing changes to a remote location, initiating a remote build, and deploying the application. A push is not limited to a single location. You could push to multiple servers simultaneously, which makes DVCS systems particularly interesting for cloud deployment. Instead of packaging your application locally and copying the result to the "cloud," you could just push the code and initiate a remote build. In a multistage environment, a successful local build could initiate a cloud push and, thus, a decentralized application deployment.

...In the Real World

I did not use the Maven deploy phase (mvn deploy) in the x-ray case. You would usually upload the result of your build into a central location and make it available to other project. The "central location" is a repository manager, such as Archiva (http://archiva.apache.org/), Nexus (http://nexus.sonatype.org/), or Artifactory (http://www.jfrog.com/), which acts as a proxy to the public Maven repository. A repository manager is used in bigger companies as a communication hub between projects. Without a repository manager, you would have to check out source code for the whole project and build everything from scratch.

Also, there is lot more to automate than what is described here. We just started with the implementation of the DevOps idea. You could create and deploy not only the application server with the installed application, but also the operating systems, virtual machines, and the whole infrastructure, for example, firewalls and other resources. Tools such as Puppet (http://www.puppetlabs.com/) or Chef (http://www.opscode.com/chef/) allow you to keep the server configuration synchronized with a central master. In the real world, you should be able to build the whole system from bare metal to running application without manual intervention.

Java EE Loves Stress and Laughs About JUnit

7

Unit tests are absolutely necessary to validate the functionality of your business logic. At the same time, the necessary surrounding infrastructure makes your life harder and slows down the execution time, so it is a good idea to mock out the inconvenient infrastructure. In production, however, your code will be executed against the real infrastructure.

The correct interaction among all components is validated during local integration tests (for example, with Arquillian) and remote integration tests. Remote integration tests are usually performed in an integration environment. Unit tests frameworks, such as JUnit (http://junit.org), are often "misused" in a good way for the implementation of a test driver. A unit test usually invokes the real (REST) service and validates the result against the expected assumptions.

Although applications always run concurrently in production, unit tests and integration tests are executed in a single thread sequentially. Contention, transaction isolation, caching behavior, memory consumption, consistency, performance, and robustness aspects, in particular, can be viably tested only under massive concurrency. The earlier you test the concurrency, the easier it is to fix the bugs.

Stress (Test) Kills Slowly

Stress tests are fun. And there is only one mission: "Kill My Server." The more load you are able to generate to "kill the server," the better.

Stress tests are great for learning about the behavior of an application server under heavy load. Memory consumption, the typical number of worker threads, the usual depth of the request queue, the number of rolled back transactions, the number of requests per second, or the number and length of major garbage collections are only a few examples of interesting runtime parameters.

You should test under heavy load not only the application server behavior, but also the implementation of your application. Memory leaks, contention points, bottlenecks, behavior of custom caches, memory consumption, and the frequency of optimistic lock exceptions are important to identify as early as possible.

In the first iteration, it is usually difficult to pass the test. You will be confronted with all kinds of small configuration and implementation challenges. It is very typical to find application, JVM, and even operating system bugs during stress tests. The earlier in the software lifecycle such bugs appear, the easier it is to fix them.

Unfortunately, in most projects, load and stress tests are still considered a "necessary evil" and they are postponed to the latest possible stage. Most of the stress tests happen shortly before going live, which makes them useless. Stress testing that is done so late is performed under time constraints and there is pressure to "pass," because there is no time left to fix possible errors. Under such circumstances, the success of the load test is more important than correctly working software or meeting the expected scalability requirements.

Finding Bugs with Stress Tests

Over time, a regularly performed stress test is a good indicator of performance degradation. Every newly implemented feature can introduce potential performance or stability problems. The more often you stress test, the better. An automated execution of stress tests at every commit would be the best possible scenario. However, a stress test takes too long and requires too many resources to be executed on every commit, so it is not really practicable. An automated stress test execution during a nightly job is a good compromise. During the first iterations, the primary goal would be to "survive the night." Later the goal would be to incrementally improve the performance and resource usage. In each case, you would get the results the next morning, and you could use them as input for planning or even refactoring.

For stress testing, x-ray was installed in a GlassFish v3.1 domain and accessed directly by Roller as well as the load driver (JMeter). No performance tunings were done; the stress test was performed on an out-of-the-box configuration.

JMeter is an easy-to-use load generator with a usable UI, as the original description states: *"Apache JMeter is open source software, a 100% pure Java desktop application designed to load test functional behavior and measure performance. It was originally designed for testing Web Applications but has since expanded to other test functions"* (http://jakarta.apache.org/jmeter/).

With JMeter, it is especially convenient to create and run HTTP load tests. JMeter can also aggregate load test data from distributed agents in real time. The x-ray API is exposed as RESTful HTTP services. X-ray was accessed by seven threads without any "think time." Two threads are dedicated for each post from the blog (`/roller/abien` and `/roller/abien/entry/`

`vegas_casino_bandits_police_and`), and they generate the statistics. The three remaining threads access the statistics (`/x-ray/resources/hitsperminute`, `/x-ray/resources/hits` and `/x-ray/resources/mostpopular`) via the REST API. My laptop was already fully utilized, so configuring more threads would not increase the load. JMeter measures the throughput, minimum, maximum, and average invocation time, and it is able to visualize the results in tables and diagrams.

I used VisualVM (http://visualvm.java.net/) to monitor the runtime behavior. VisualVM gives you some insights into the JVM behavior and is described as *"…a visual tool integrating several commandline JDK tools and lightweight profiling capabilities. Designed for both production and development time use, it further enhances the capability of monitoring and performance analysis for the Java SE platform…"*

VisualVM is currently bundled with JDK 1.6, but it is worth using the more recent versions from the VisualVM Web site.

During the stress test, I used VisualVM to monitor the GlassFish JVM. Particularly interesting was information about the memory consumption, number of threads, and CPU utilization. The VisualVM-MBeans plug-in allows you to integrate JMX MBean view and it makes JConsole obsolete. Visual GC is useful for visualizing Garbage Collector activities during stress tests. Both plug-ins were installed with the plug-in manager.

...and How Did It Perform?

X-ray performance turned out to be five times better than Roller weblogger. X-ray was able to handle more than 1.5k transactions per second, and Roller was less than 50 transactions per second. There are about 15k visitors a day on my blog, so x-ray could handle the load in 10 seconds :-).

Label	# Samples	Average	Median	90% Line	Min	Max	Error %	Throughput	KB/se
AccessTotal...	159247	4	3	10	0	219	0.00%	409.1/sec	
AccessHitsP...	184429	3	2	9	0	230	0.00%	473.8/sec	
HitsPerHour	183199	3	2	9	0	268	0.00%	470.7/sec	
/roller/abien	18258	25	24	35	11	215	0.00%	46.9/sec	33
Vegas Post	18258	16	15	23	3	148	0.01%	46.9/sec	21
TOTAL	563391	5	2	14	0	268	0.00%	1447.4/sec	55

Figure 7: JMeter Setup and Performance Results

It is important to note that every page view also initiates several REST requests to the

153

backend, so the actual throughput was even higher. During the duration of the stress tests (approximately half an hour), no jobs were rejected and so no statistics were lost. The slowest POST request took 52 ms. The overall performance was acceptable as well. Only the asynchronous cache flushing took about 4 seconds (see Listing 84). All other methods were performed in less than one second.

```xml
<invocations>

<invocation methodName="public void
com.abien.xray.business.store.control.PersistentStore.store
(java.util.Map)" invocationPerformance="3935"/>

<invocation methodName="public void
com.abien.xray.business.store.boundary.Hits.persistReferersCache()"
invocationPerformance="3935"/>

<invocation methodName="public java.util.Map
com.abien.xray.business.store.control.PersistentRefererStore.getRefere
rs()" invocationPerformance="1046"/>

<invocation methodName="public java.util.Map
com.abien.xray.business.store.control.PersistentHitStore.getHits()"
invocationPerformance="200"/>

<invocation methodName="public java.lang.String
com.abien.xray.business.store.boundary.HitsResource.totalHitsAsString
()" invocationPerformance="102"/>

<invocation methodName="public java.lang.String
com.abien.xray.business.store.boundary.Hits.totalHitsAsString()"
invocationPerformance="102"/>

<invocation methodName="public java.util.List
com.abien.xray.business.store.boundary.MostPopular.totalHitsAsString
(int)" invocationPerformance="100"/>

<invocation methodName="public java.util.List
com.abien.xray.business.store.control.PersistentHitStore.getMostPopula
rPosts(int)" invocationPerformance="98"/>

<invocation methodName="public void
com.abien.xray.business.store.boundary.Hits.persistHitsCache()"
invocationPerformance="10"/><invocation methodName="public void
com.abien.xray.business.store.boundary.Hits.resetTrends()"
invocationPerformance="7"/>

<invocation methodName="public long
com.abien.xray.business.store.boundary.Hits.totalHits()"
invocationPerformance="2"/>

</invocations>
```

Listing 84: Slowest Methods During Stress Test

GlassFish allocated 130 MB of RAM during the stress tests and used thirteen more threads (Live Peak 89) than in the idle state (see Figure 8).

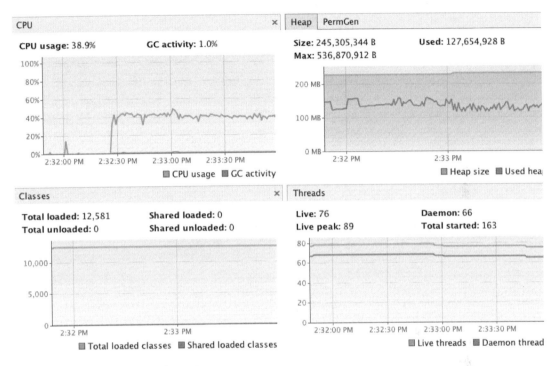

Figure 8: Monitoring VisualVM Output

Only two major garbage collections occurred during the load tests and they were performed in 1.4 seconds.

Lessons Learned

Stress tests are perfectly suitable for the identification of bottlenecks, validation of "suspicious" parts of the system, and robustness testing. Memory leaks, deadlocks, and contention points often appear only under heavy load and they are hard to identify in single-threaded unit tests or integration tests. Pragmatic stress tests are also the most convenient way to estimate runtime behavior and necessary resources such as RAM, CPUs, and the number of nodes to handle the necessary throughput.

Load generation is important, but the availability of performance and monitoring probes is essential for the evaluation and interpretation of results. X-ray comes with JMX and REST monitoring. I used both to monitor the state of the system. It was easy to identify the slowest methods of the system or the current state of the cache. Application-specific probes significantly increase the (stress) testability of the system. With VisualVM sampler, the overhead for monitoring could be identified easily as well (it was about 1%).

JDK 1.6 and Java EE application servers come with interesting monitoring probes already. Especially interesting for stability and robustness tests are the following parameters:

- Current size of the heap

- Current number of threads and peak number of threads

- Number of successful transactions

- Number of rolled-back transactions

- Garbage Collector activity

- Number of requests in the queue

- Number of database connections

- Size of the JPA caches

Robustness and stability are the actual goal of stress testing. In this context, all the values listed above should also be "stable." There should be no increase of memory, threads, or uncontrolled cache growth over time. Also performance degradation would indicate a potential resource problem. In general, all the measured values should have a modest progression. Random peaks or degradations are usually early indicators of potential problems.

X-ray was built with many enterprise features such as JAX-RS, EJB 3.1, interceptors, CDI managed beans, events, timers, and JPA entities. Performance and scalability were not the main drivers behind x-ray's architecture; rather, simplicity and maintainability were the main drivers. The heavy use of enterprise features didn't sacrifice good performance. It turns out, the overhead for using containers and, particularly, EJB beans, CDI managed beans, and interceptors, is hardly measurable
(see http://www.adam-bien.com/roller/abien/entry/dependency_injection_performance_in_java). Premature optimization and replacement of EJB beans or CDI managed beans just leads to code bloat (http://www.adam-bien.com/roller/abien/entry/jsf_jpa_ejb_bloat) and doesn't have any measurable effect on performance.

Regardless how good the performance of EJB beans, CDI, JAX-RS, and JPA is, overall performance is highly dependent on the container implementation. Extensive stress tests not only measure the performance; they also verify robustness and stability. Every new application server release can have a negative impact on the non-functional requirements described here.

Entity Control Boundary: Perhaps the Simplest Possible Architecture

8

The way in which architectures are created in Java EE 6 is fundamentally different than the way they are created in J2EE. The J2EE programming model was (it's already 8 years old...) intrusive and required the heavy use of interfaces and checked exceptions. A strict separation between business logic and infrastructure was not provided. You had to start with a set of patterns such as Business Delegate, Service Locator, Session Façade, or Data Transfer Object just to implement trivial applications in a reasonable way.

Inversion of Thinking

Java EE 6 is different. There are no required dependencies on the platform except metadata in the form of annotations or XML. In Java EE 6, the infrastructure is already cleanly separated by design. Patterns and "best practices" are needed only to solve application- or domain-specific challenges, not to solve platform issues.

Not only the control was inverted in Java EE (see "Inversion of Control," http://en.wikipedia.org/wiki/Inversion_of_control). The process of creating architectures was inverted as well. In J2EE, you usually started with patterns, layers, and indirections, and then you started to analyze the business logic—a typical top-down approach. In Java EE 6, there is no need for upfront design. You can start with the realization of business logic and introduce patterns and best practices on demand.

Business Components

Java EE does a good job of separating the business logic from the infrastructure. You can concentrate fully on the realization of domain logic and almost ignore the Java EE platform. Usually, you start by analyzing the target domain data, which results in domain objects or entities.

Entities with similar responsibilities are organized in packages. Such a package is named either by abstracting the responsibilities of all included entities or by using the name of the most important entity.

In later iterations, you extend the package with reusable services (the "control") and a dedicated service interface to the outside world (the "boundary"). A package named by its domain responsibilities with dedicated external interfaces is a business component. It is created according to the "Maximal Cohesion, Minimal Coupling" principle. All containing elements inside a business component should have similar responsibilities, but different components should be as loosely coupled as possible. Some business components do not need to maintain any (persistent) state and so as entities, they are created considering the responsibilities of controls and boundaries.

X-ray comes with seven business components:

- configuration: Responsible for centralizing configuration in one place and consists of boundary and control.

- logging: Responsible for creation and injection of loggers and comprises a single boundary package.

- maintenance: Comprises only a single subpackage: the boundary. Manages caches and returns the current version.

- monitoring: Responsible for exposing runtime data, such as the number of exceptions and the slowest methods, and providing access to diagnostic data. The business component monitoring consists of the boundary and entity layer. The entities are transient and used only for JSON/XML serialization.

- statistics: Exposes daily, hourly, and minutely statistics. Contains the boundary and entity layers. The entities are transient.

- store: The core business logic. Manages the hit and referer caches and computes the statistics. It contains all three layers (entity, control, and boundary).

- useragent: Computes user agent (browser) statistics and contains all three layers.

Most of the components are dependent on the logging functionality; some need a reference to the Hits boundary. The CDI event mechanism was used to decouple business components and get rid of superfluous coupling. X-ray components are a perfect example of the "Maximal Cohesion, Minimal Coupling" idea. The example, however, is rather unrealistic. The strict decoupling between components is possible only because there are no relations between persistent entities. In more complex scenarios, you will have to deal with cross-component persistent relations between entities. Either you will have to cut persistent relations between entities and give up joins, or you will have to take dependencies between components into consideration.

Entity Control Boundary

Although most of the J2EE patterns are superfluous (see *Real World Java EE Patterns—Rethinking Best Practices*, http://press.adam-bien.com), a minimal structure does significantly improve maintainability. The Entity Control Boundary (ECB) pattern is similar to Model–View–Controller (MVC), but it is not applicable only for the UI (http://epf.eclipse.org/wikis/openuppt/openup_basic/guidances/concepts/entity_control_boundary_pattern,_uF-QYEAhEdq_UJTvM1DM2Q.html). ECB is older than the Unified Modeling Language (UML) and it is supported by most design tools. Each element of the ECB pattern comes with its own icon (see Figure 9).

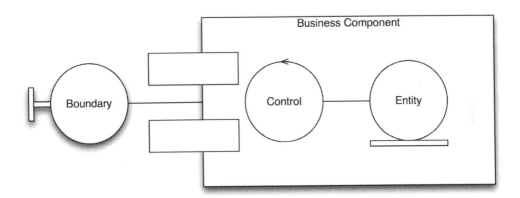

Figure 9: Structure of the ECB Pattern

The ECB pattern is used for the creation of layers inside the business component with the same name. Every component contains boundary, control, and entity subpackages. At a minimum, the boundary package is required. CRUD functionality can be realized with just a boundary and entity layers. Realization of more sophisticated business logic usually requires all three layers.

Boundary

Boundary exposes the implementation of a business component to the outside world. The main responsibility is to provide, as conveniently as possible, access to the functionality hidden

159

behind the boundary. A boundary is coarse grained, and makes "business sense" to its user. The class `com.abien.xray.business.store.boundary.HitsResource` exposes an easy-to-use REST interface and does not reveal any details about its implementation:

```
@PUT

@Consumes({MediaType.TEXT_PLAIN})

    public Response updateStatistics(@Context HttpHeaders httpHeaders,
String url) {

}
```

Extraction, filtering, and storage are implemented in the `com.abien.xray.business.store.boundary.Hits` class, which is independent of REST and HTTP. The protocol-agnostic method `Hits#updateStatistics` is invoked by the `HitsResource` EJB bean:

```
    public void updateStatistics(String uri, String referer,
Map<String, String> headerMap) {}
```

The `Hits` EJB bean orchestrates controls, such as `HitsCache`, `PersistentHitStore`, `PersistentRefererStore`, or `TitleFetcher`, to implement the exposed functionality. All controls were introduced afterwards to decrease the boundary complexity and increase its cohesion.

The boundary in the `storage` business component consists of two parts: the `Hits` and `HitsResource` classes. `HitResource` is heavily JAX-RS dependent, but it does not implement any business logic. The EJB bean `Hits`, on the other hand, is only responsible for providing the exposed functionality and it is highly protocol agnostic. Splitting a boundary into two halves increases testability and makes the business logic protocol agnostic. Consequently, you will need a dedicated "protocol boundary" for each exposed protocol, such as Hessian, SOAP, or Google Web Toolkit Remote Procedure Call (GWT RPC). The protocol-agnostic part should be able to handle all protocols without any change.

Control

A control implements parts of business logic that are coordinated by a boundary. A control is usually finer than a boundary and does not appear as a standalone use case. A control is a product of refactoring and, in particular, "Separation of Concerns." A control represents a part of the business logic realized by a boundary and is, therefore, less interesting for external use.

In Java EE 6, a control is an optional artifact. Simple CRUD cases can be conveniently implemented with a boundary (with injected `EntityManager`) and an entity. Control is a product of refactoring and, in particular, the "divide and conquer" idea

160

(http://en.wikipedia.org/wiki/Divide_and_conquer_algorithm). In the bottom-up Java EE 6 approach, controls are created after a few iterations. A boundary grows until it becomes unmanageable and is no longer cohesive. Part of the functionality is factored out into a new control and, thus, the next layer. All controls from the `storage` component (`HitsCache`, `InMemoryTitleCache`, `HttpHeaderFilter`, and so on) were created during a refactoring phase.

A control never starts a new transaction. It is always invoked by a boundary within an active transaction context.

Entity

An entity is just an object with persistent state. An object is defined as follows: *"…In the domain of object-oriented programming an object is usually taken to mean a compilation of attributes (object elements) and behaviors (methods or subroutines) encapsulating an entity…"* (http://en.wikipedia.org/wiki/Object_(computer_science)). This definition perfectly fits the description of an entity.

Because we tend to use the name "object" for things that are actually not objects, for example, data structures without behavior such as DTO (http://en.wikipedia.org/wiki/Data_transfer_object), or procedures without state, such as DAO http://en.wikipedia.org/wiki/Data_access_object), a "rich domain object" is a far better definition for an entity.

An entity maintains state, which is usually persistent. Persistent entities in Java EE 6 usually rely on the JPA 2 specification for mapping their state to a database table. Because of the limitations in Container-Managed Persistence (CMP) (http://java.sun.com/developer/technicalArticles/ebeans/EJB20CMP/) in J2EE, as well as J2EE's intrusive programming model, entities in J2EE were mostly anemic. Without support for inheritance and the polymorphic behavior, any implementation of business logic inside entities had only drawbacks. You couldn't leverage the full power of objects, and your logic was dependent on the CMP infrastructure.

In Java EE 6, the opposite is best practice. JPA 2 entities are domain objects that can be persisted with just a few annotations and without any further dependency on the JPA API. The persistent entity `Hit` implements formatting, and the transient `Post` entity shortens titles and implements the `java.lang.Comparable` interface (see Listing 85).

```
@Entity
public class Hit {
    //...
    public String getActionId() {
```

```java
        if(actionId == null){
            return null;
        }
        if(actionId.startsWith("/entry")){
            return trimTrailingSlash(actionId);
        }


        return actionId;
    }


    public final String trimTrailingSlash(String actionId) {
        if(actionId != null && actionId.endsWith("/")){
            return actionId.substring(0, actionId.length()-1);
        }
        return actionId;
    }
}
public class Post implements Comparable<Post>{
//…
    public String getShortenedTitle(int totalLength){
        if(title == null){
            return null;
        }
        int length = title.length();
        if(length < totalLength){
            return title;
        }
        String shortened = title.substring(0, totalLength - 5);
        return shortened + "[...]";
    }
```

```
@Override

public int compareTo(Post other) {

    if(numberOfHits == other.numberOfHits){

        return 0;

    }

    if(numberOfHits > other.numberOfHits){

        return 1;

    }

    return -1;

}

}
```

Listing 85: Entities with Domain Logic

Even this simplistic case significantly improves the maintainability and decreases the total amount of code. The entities are more testable, the business logic is encapsulated, and there is no need to introduce another session bean (control) to implement business logic. In Java EE 6, "Anemic Domain Models" are not only considered to be potentially "code smell" (http://en.wikipedia.org/wiki/Code_smell), as Martin Fowler states: "…*In general, the more behavior you find in the services, the more likely you are to be robbing yourself of the benefits of a domain model. If all your logic is in services, you've robbed yourself blind*" (http://www.martinfowler.com/bliki/AnemicDomainModel.html).

Some Statistics

9

In this chapter, I would like to share some unrelated x-ray services statistics to give you an idea about Java EE 6 behavior, deployment requirements, and runtime "overhead." Java EE 6 is still judged with the experience in mind from its 8-year-old predecessor, J2EE 1.4. In practice, Java EE 6 is even leaner than its "competitors."

Size of the deployment archive (`x-ray.war` = x-ray-services)	76 KB
Size of the x-ray probe Roller plug-in (REST client and Roller integration)	28 KB
Size of the Roller 4 deployment archive (`roller.war`); everything is bundled with the WAR file; no Java EE 6 functionality (such as JPA, EJB, and so) on is used	24 MB
Duration of a full deployment on GlassFish 3.1 (`asadmin` from the command line)	3.2 seconds
Duration of a full domain installation with resources (`asadmin` from the command line)	26 seconds
Duration of full Maven 3 build with Scala	26 seconds
Duration of full Maven 3 build without Scala	5 seconds

Max number of transactions per second (TX), which is writes/hits, on a single node, without any optimization	1.400 TX
Max number of transaction per day (writes/hits)	120.960.000 TX
Number of hits in 24 hours (was handled in ~10 seconds during a load test)	10.000 – 20.000
Average number of cached referers	65.000
Average number of dirty referers (60 seconds)	~5000
Average number of cached hits	3500
Average number of dirty hits (60 seconds)	~10
Slowest x-ray response time (over REST/HTTP)	820 ms
Average x-ray response time (over REST/HTTP)	1-10 ms
Slowest method invocation	1254 ms
Top five slowest methods	`Hits.persistReferersCache` [1254 ms] `PersistentStore.store (java.util.Map)` [1252 ms] `PersistentRefererStore.getReferers()` [927 ms] `MostPopular.totalHitsAsString (int)` [735 ms] `PersistentHitStore.getMostPopularPosts(int)` [734 ms]
Average RAM consumption	115 MB
Average number of threads	73
Peak number of threads	92
Total number of classes (production + test)	58

Number of interfaces	5

Interfaces	`XRayMonitoringMBean`
	`XRayLogger`
	`ConfigurationProvider`
	`MonitoringResourceMXBean`
	`TitleCache`

Number of XML files	2 (`beans.xml` and `persistence.xml`)
Number of XML lines of code	14 (`persistence.xml`) + 1 (`beans.xml`) = 15
Total lines of code	2645
Number of production classes (`src/main/java`)	46
Lines of code of production classes (`src/main/java`)	551
Estimated man-days	3–5 days total; first "production release" took 1 day
Number of GlassFish-specific dependencies	0
Fun factor (1–10)	11 :-)

Made in the USA
San Bernardino, CA
27 December 2013